OPERATIONS
OFFICER'S
GUIDE

TITLES IN THE SERIES

THE U.S. NAVAL INSTITUTE BLUE & GOLD
PROFESSIONAL LIBRARY

FOR MORE THAN 100 YEARS, U.S. NAVY PROFESSIONALS have counted on specialized books published by the Naval Institute Press to prepare them for their responsibilities as they advance in their careers and to serve as ready references and refreshers when needed. From the days of coal-fired battleships to the era of unmanned aerial vehicles and laser weaponry, such perennials as *The Bluejacket's Manual* and the *Watch Officer's Guide* have guided generations of Sailors through the complex challenges of naval service. As these books are updated and new ones are added to the list, they will carry the distinctive mark of the Blue and Gold Professional Library series to remind and reassure their users that they have been prepared by naval professionals and meet the exacting standards that sailors have long expected from the U.S. Naval Institute.

BLUE & GOLD
PROFESSIONAL LIBRARY

OPERATIONS OFFICER'S GUIDE

CDR JOHN R. H. CALLAWAY, USN

NAVAL INSTITUTE PRESS
ANNAPOLIS, MARYLAND

Naval Institute Press
291 Wood Road
Annapolis, MD 21402

Library of Congress Cataloging-in-Publication Data

Callaway, John.
  Operations officer's guide / John Callaway.
     p. cm.
  ISBN 978-1-59114-111-2 (hbk. : alk. paper) 1. United States. Navy—Officers' handbooks. 2. Naval art and science—United States. I. Title.
  V133.C35 2012
  359.00973—dc23

                                                                    2011051959

♾ This paper meets the requirements of ANSI/NISO z39.48-1992 (Permanence of Paper).

Printed in the United States of America.

20 19 18 17 16 15 14 13 12   9 8 7 6 5 4 3 2 1
First printing

CONTENTS

ACKNOWLEDGMENTS

THANKS TO ALL THE OFFICERS, CHIEF PETTY OFFICERS, AND sailors I served with during my sea tours. The scope and depth of this book are testament to their abilities and our shared experiences. The limitations, errors and omissions of the book are mine. Although I am in debt to many for training and educating me through my career, I consider Commander Al Carver (now retired) my first and foremost mentor and friend. He was also the first to review this manuscript and I value his counsel above all others. Lieutenant Commander Warren Smith, Lieutenant Commander Johnny Graves, and Lieutenant Craig "Mac" MacDonald are also close friends and true operations professionals who contributed immensely to this book. I look forward to feedback from the Fleet to improve this work and maintain its relevance for those who serve as operations officers.

INTRODUCTION

THIS BOOK IS PRIMARILY A PRACTICAL GUIDE to leading and managing the operations department aboard a United States Navy warship. It is written for the operations officer who leads the department, but is also a useful tool for anyone interested in how the fleet works. To succeed in today's Navy the operations officer must understand the global environment in which it operates, as well as the organizational context of how Navy missions are defined and assigned.

THE GLOBAL ENVIRONMENT

Often referred to simply as "Ops," the operations officer occupies an incredibly challenging and rewarding position that requires dynamic leadership and management skills. Every ship (and every staff) in the fleet needs good operations officers.

More than thirty years ago, Captain P. T. Deutermann wrote *The Ops Officer Manual*, an important reference that covered everything from planning to wartime operations. To say that the world and the Navy are different in the post–Cold War, post–September 11 environment of today is a monumental understatement. The disintegration of our Soviet rival and the emergence of the terrorist threat changed the battle group orientation of Cold War deployments to the more dispersed tasking of today. Revolutions in communications and military technology combined with the fleet's reduction in size make each ship exponentially more important, and, necessarily, more capable.

In today's Navy individual ships—and therefore the operations officers who plan, coordinate, and execute their tasking—more often operate independently. Navy ships have traditionally been the standard-bearers for American diplomacy, the keepers of customary international law, and the most militarily capable force on the seas. Today's U.S. Navy ships are also the executive nodes of a networked architecture wielding the soft power of forward presence, the persistent "eyes and ears" of intelligence, surveillance, and reconnaissance, and the destructive capabilities of our power projection.

The operations officer's importance is appreciated beyond the U.S. Navy. In October 2003 the Chinese Navy ship *Shenzen* visited Guam with the commander of the East Sea Fleet embarked. During a formal luncheon on the second day of the visit, a senior Chinese Navy captain leaned over to the lone American lieutenant—the most junior person in the room—and inquired about his job. After considering the lieutenant's response, the Chinese captain exclaimed: "Operations Officer...*very* important person." Hardly a Confucian aphorism, his comment nevertheless was to me, the ship's operations officer, explicit recognition of a key position. In today's global environment the ops officer must be fully cognizant of geopolitical sensitivities, intelligence requirements, and operational law in addition to the traditional attributes of leadership, seamanship, management skill, and tactical ability.

THE MISSION

In its broadest terms a U.S. Navy ship's mission is to conduct prompt and sustained combat operations at sea. Colloquially, we refer to this as warfighting. "A Cooperative Strategy for 21st Century Seapower," our nation's maritime strategy, lists six Navy missions: forward presence, deterrence, sea control, power projection, maritime security, and humanitarian assistance and disaster response. The capabilities needed for these various missions are derived from warfighting capabilities developed to conduct combat operations. Such adaptability makes Navy ships inherently capable of multiple missions and uniquely flexible among military units. The Navy designs each ship from the keel up based on required operational capabilities and a projected operating environment. The specific missions required for each ship are described in training instructions as "warfare areas." Warfare areas include the spectrum of air, surface, and antisubmarine capabilities to noncombat, mission-essential tasks such as flight operations, logistics, and medical support. When an operational commander needs a ship to conduct a mission, he or she reviews that ship's readiness in the desired warfare areas. If satisfactory, it receives the operational tasking.

The Surface Forces Training Manual details the capabilities that ships need for each warfare area, and sets standards for training. The manning, material, and training requirements associated with the warfare areas are then formally reported to the operational commander. The ship's superiors review communications from its various departments and the operational commander determines if the ship can or should be tasked with a particular mission. It is the operations officer's job to ensure that the chain of command has a clear picture of the ship's readiness. In summary, to complete its mission, the ship must be tasked; to be tasked, the ship must be ready; to be ready, the ship's crew must train. Ops stands at the nexus of the ship and the fleet for providing a trained and ready ship for mission tasking.

THE BOOK

This book goes beyond the mechanics of operations officer duties to discuss leadership opportunities and management techniques applicable to the operations officers of our diverse and sophisticated fleet. First and foremost, it is designed as a preparation guide for officers detailed to the operations officer billet, whether second-tour division officers assigned to minesweepers or second-tour department heads assigned to major commands. As you prepare for your tour, this book will frame the wide scope of the job and help you ask the right questions. It will also serve as a useful reference for all operations department personnel, from those trying to figure out the complex organization in which they work to senior enlisted leaders broadening their knowledge of the department and the ship.

Much literature has been devoted to understanding and defining leadership, management, and the difference between the two. This book emphasizes the need for both and divides them roughly between actions of execution (management) and actions of inspiration (leadership). Sometimes, an action can be both. Chapters 1, 3, 5, and 7 primarily address leadership networks, training, routine operations, and deployment. Chapters 2, 4, 6, and 8 focus mainly on the management of schedules, department routines, administration, and collateral duties. Chapter 9 ties the leadership opportunities and management skills discussed in the book together to broaden the perspective of the operations officer beyond the department, with an eye toward command.

To highlight important "takeaways," I have begun each chapter with a list of key lessons under the heading "The Bottom Line Up Front," or "BLUF." Each chapter ends with a similarly helpful, bulleted section of "Professional Tips," which includes time-savers, organizational tools, and otherwise useful advice pulled from the chapters for quick reference.

The book's appendixes offer examples of resources not easily found elsewhere. The first, which exhibits a force tactical action officer letter, captures some of the book's themes and suggests a qualification to which one might aspire. The second appendix is a template instruction for a ship information security program. Mandated by the Department of Defense, the Navy is currently implementing this program at the unit level. Appendix C is an operations security (OPSEC) notification. Finally, a tailored glossary is provided as a quick reference to key terms that Ops will regularly encounter.

It is my sincere hope that this book assists the Navy in developing a fundamentally sound cadre of operations officers. Feedback to the author through the U.S. Naval Institute is appreciated.

PROFESSIONAL TIPS:

■ Read "A Cooperative Strategy for 21st Century Seapower" (www.navy.mil/maritime/Maritimestrategy.pdf), accessed July 2011.

■ Each ship class has its own Required Operational Capability/ Projected Operating Environment (ROC/POE) document. For example, the ROC/POE for cruisers is Chief of Naval Operations Instruction 3501.160B, Required Operational Capability/Projected Operating Environment for CG-47 (*Ticonderoga*-class) Guided Missile Cruisers. Read your ship's ROC/POE.

■ The Surface Force Training Manual is Commander, Naval Surface Forces Instruction 3502.1D (Change 2) dated January 27, 2010. This key reference is hereafter abbreviated as SFTM. It is often pronounced "sir-for-tray-man."

■ Another good resource document is Naval Doctrine Publication 1, *Naval Warfare*. Sister document to the "Cooperative Strategy for 21st Century Seapower," it provides our Navy's fundamental operating principles.

CHAPTER 1

PROFESSIONAL NETWORKS

BLUF:

- *Professional relationships are the bases for leadership opportunities.*
- *Professional networks are the conduits for mission accomplishment.*

USS CHANCELLORSVILLE Operations Department officers
and chief petty officers, 2004.
Author's collection.

As mentioned in the introduction, the operations officer is the primary interface between the ship and rest of the Navy. The Navy—particularly that portion at the task force level—is becoming a "flatter" network in which current operations and logistics are dynamic and openly discussed across organizations and even international coalitions. Within its lifelines, the ship's chain of command continues to be more hierarchical—a rigid type of management structure that, if out of vogue in business and academic circles, is proven and effective on Navy ships. Current management theory heralds free flows of information and insists that only a "flat," informal organization can achieve necessary information sharing. However, favorable information flows and hierarchical structures are not mutually exclusive. The inflexibility of the ship's organizational structure comes from a framework designed for rapid decision making and execution in times of shipboard emergency and war through effective delegation and accountability. The command climate need not be rigid at all; in fact, the Navy encourages free information flow. The best ships cultivate a culture of feedback and innovation that values questioning attitudes, honest debriefs, and forceful backup.

PART I: Networks Inside the Lifelines: Leading the Operations Department

A ship's chain of command stretches from the newest sailor all the way up to the captain, the commanding officer (CO). As one of the line department heads, the operations officer plays a pivotal role in it. The CO relies on this officer to lead and manage roughly a third of the crew, in addition to acting as the conduit for the bulk of off-ship communication. Ops leads a departmental structure that includes junior officers, chief petty officers, and sailors.

The Command Triad

Leadership on any ship starts with the commanding officer, who is clearly charged with the authority and responsibility to run it. To be effective the operations officer must develop a strong relationship with the CO. This starts with understanding the CO's priorities. Ops is most effective within the squadron or task force if allowed to speak authoritatively about the ship's schedule and make commitments on the spot. Delegated by the CO, this authority must be exercised judiciously. Ops may also represent the CO in meetings ranging from informal conversations to warfare commanders' conferences. It should be the goal of every operations officer to gain the trust and confidence of the CO, particularly with regard to the ship's schedule.

The relationship between the CO and Ops is formed during the turnover process, whether the CO is turning over command or Ops is new to the ship. If the former, Ops should be completely forthright as to where the department stands. If the latter, the new operations officer should conduct a thorough review of all department programs and processes. Commend the out-going operations officer where warranted and present a plan to address any challenges. About a month after turnover, conduct a fresh review of how things are going and reassess the department's priorities. Detail (in a memo or e-mail, depending upon your CO) your perspective since assuming your duties, and briefly summarize your long-range goals and plans as well as where you will focus your energies. This second assessment will give the CO an updated view of the department and allow for course corrections or realignment of priorities.

The executive officer (or XO) is second in command and responsible for the administration of the ship and execution of the daily routine. The key to a successful relationship with the XO is conducting a meaningful Planning Board For Training (PBFT)—a weekly meeting in which the executive officer, command master chief, and department heads lay out the ship's internal schedule for the upcoming two weeks and discuss long-range plans. The primary product of each PBFT is a two-week schedule from which the XO extracts the daily schedule. Ops should receive input from fellow department heads and executive assistants prior to the PBFT in order to keep it short and productive.

According to the Standard Organization and Regulations of the U.S. Navy (SORN) manual, department heads report to the XO only for administration and should report directly to the CO for operational matters. It is imperative, however, to keep the XO informed about important department activities, especially matters regarding the ship's schedule. First, the XO is a senior, experienced surface warfare officer keenly interested in the ship's success. The XO is also likely to become the CO in the new fleet-up progression, in which an officer serves as XO and then CO on the same ship in consecutive tours.

Typically a command senior chief or command master chief, the command's senior enlisted leader (SEL) is the third leg of a ship's "command triad." As such, it is important for every department head to have a working relationship with the SEL. Ops can support the latter's relationships with crew members and their families by sharing scheduling information with the SEL in the same way as do the other department heads. The SEL supports the operations officer by taking care of Ops' sailors, mentoring the chief petty officers, and providing advice.

Fellow Department Heads

Ops' fellow department heads typically include a supply officer and an engineer officer, as well as a weapons officer, a combat systems officer, or, on amphibious ships, a first lieutenant. The working relationship between department heads is the only flat part of the shipboard network—a small group of peers that must interact well for the ship to run efficiently, especially in environments in which the ship faces multiple demands. Information sharing is key. Ops must receive scheduling input from the other department heads and coordinate them for presentation to the XO during the PBFT. Team effort, meanwhile, is essential to scheduling all the required and sometimes conflicting events. If deprived of the department heads' input, Ops must fall back on the requirements laid out in the SFTM, Joint Fleet Maintenance Manual, and other references. While these sources generally provide Ops with sufficient information, the department that does not provide input is driven by Ops and may balk at the schedule (or even try to ignore it).

The best way for department heads to resolve conflicts, gather input, and generally remain on the same page is to talk on a regular basis. For example, a brief meeting over a cup of coffee while everyone else is at divisional quarters can be collegial and productive. This type of interaction is typically initiated by the senior line department head or senior watch officer (SWO). Regardless of who initiates the conversations or how they are conducted, Ops should share with all other department heads the best information available regarding the ship's schedules and off-ship interactions. A leadership opportunity that sets the tone for cooperation across department lines, this can only benefit the ship as a whole. Another practical way to share information is ensuring that the department is represented at your counterparts' coordination meetings—Planning Board For Maintenance, for example. Being transparent builds required trust among equals. Whatever the mechanism, a team-building approach goes a long way in assuring success for all.

Operations Departmental Leading Chief Petty Officer

The departmental leading chief petty officer (LCPO) position is not clearly defined in the SORN, but it represents a leadership opportunity to develop subordinates and promote trust within the department. One way for Ops to develop a strong departmental LCPO is to model your relationship with that officer after that of a CO and senior enlisted leader (SEL). Traditionally the most senior department chief petty officer (with a strong role in the chief petty officer's mess), the departmental LCPO may simply be the most willing or the most talented of the department's assigned chiefs. The LCPO works closely with the SEL, and sits on command boards such as the disciplinary review board and sailor of the quarter board. The departmental LCPO may be encouraged to expand the role and assist Ops with discipline, recognition, evaluations, and advancement within the department. Meeting regularly with the LCPO is a good practice that can promote mutual trust, provide insight into the department from both perspectives, and pay big dividends. These meetings need not be formal or separate from other activities. For example, walk through departmental berthing areas and discuss your sailors' concerns or long-range goals.

Operations Limited Duty Officers/Chief Warrant Officers

Some ships are staffed with operations limited duty officers (LDOs) or chief warrant officers (CWOs). LDOs and CWOs are technical specialists who, as enlisted sailors, typically demonstrated superior skills and an aptitude for more complex, operations-related work. Capable, experienced, and hard-working, these unabashed "workaholics" make potentially powerful workhorses for the department. Take full advantage of their expertise, but also challenge them to work at the warfare commander level. LDOs and CWOs can fill roles from division officer to assistant department head. Often they are employed in their area of expertise, as in the case of air defense officers. Employing your key assistants is a leadership opportunity for you and potentially for them. LDOs have a different career path than line officers so check with senior LDOs or contact their detailer to find out how to take care of LDOs in their fitness reports.

Second-Tour Division Officers

With the experience of a previous ship tour under their belts, these young officers have completed their basic qualifications.

During this second tour they assume greater responsibility and work toward more advanced qualification, typically while serving as training officer, navigator, or in other, similar roles. One or both of these officers may be assigned to the operations department. The training officer's and navigator's duties are closely aligned with those of Ops, and present yet another leadership opportunity for developing subordinates. Officers assigned to second-tour positions are generally very capable and should be groomed for their future role as department heads. One way to encourage and prepare them is to cultivate a "near-peer" relationship by including them in department head–level planning and decision making. Remember, your most important job is to train the next generation of junior officers for department head assignment. You may be training your own relief.

First-Tour Division Officers

For future operations officers, indeed all department heads, broad experience as division officers, regardless of billet assignment, is imperative for professional development. Such officers should learn to draft messages, conduct briefings, manage programs, coordinate inspections or events, participate in ship's evolutions, and stand watch topside.

In recent years the Navy has sent greater numbers of young ensigns straight to the fleet. Their training can be approached in a number of ways: One is to keep them out of division officer assignments until they achieve basic qualifications. Another is to assign them as junior division officers (see SORN, 3-152) so they can be mentored by more experienced division officers. Each approach involves its own degree of formality, and it seems that no two ships handle the assignment the same way. However, best practices include assigning responsibilities to the ensigns quickly and clearly and directly involving more senior officers in their qualification processes.

The department head always needs to be involved with the training of first-tour division officers, because they will serve as the department's "middle management." And their progress toward qualification contributes significantly to their job satisfaction. While the commanding officer and senior watch officer are responsible for timely qualification of junior officers, the department head should take advantage of this leadership opportunity to mentor and train.

Chief Petty Officers

Chief petty officers are the technical experts and mid-level managers who run each division. The effectiveness of fundamental programs such as training, maintenance, safety, damage control, cleanliness, etc., is based on the chiefs' performance. There is a strong correlation between effective chief petty officer leadership and being out "on the deckplates." Lead by example and make your expectations in this regard known.

The toughest lesson for a department head to learn is when and how to confront a chief petty officer. Typically, chiefs are technical experts with at least as much if not significantly more sea time (experience at sea) than the department head. But they can still be wrong. Department heads should expect to need to align management styles and handle disagreements with a chief at some point during their two tours. Assessing the situation, seeking advice from the command master chief, and developing a strategy for empowering chiefs in a way that furthers your goals are formative leadership experiences on the way to command.

First Class Petty Officers/Leading Petty Officers

The next generation of chief petty officers, first class petty officers (known simply as "first class") are not there yet. Challenge them to run the daily routine, starting with morning quarters. The morning "call to quarters" is a Navy tradition with three parts: muster, instruction, and inspection. Task the first class to conduct all three elements daily. The SORN clearly states the responsibilities of divisional, leading petty officers. Pay special attention to the training aspect of their duties. Everything from general military training to advancement studies can be handled at their level. Encourage them to rise to the challenge and mentor those who do not. One good practice is to meet quarterly with the first class petty officers. Bring along the departmental LCPO and encourage an open discussion. You may learn something about the department that you need to know.

PART II: Networks Outside the Lifelines: Advocating for Your Ship

The operations officer must actively manage two off-ship networks. One supports the ship's readiness; the other is a "consumer" of that readiness. The administrative chain of command is responsible for manning, training, and equipping the force. The operational chain of command is responsible for executing the Navy's mission. Navy staffs in both chains typically use a common nomenclature. While Navy organizations vary (and are occasionally combined) depending on size and mission, they generally operate as the following:

> N1 is administration and personnel.
> N2 is intelligence.
> N3 is operations.
> N4 is logistics.
> N5 is plans.
> N6 is communications.
> N7 is exercises or training.
> N8 is resources or readiness.

Often these offices will be referred to as "N-codes." Joint (representation from all U.S. military services) and combined (representation from allied or coalition) staffs will be similarly organized, but with a *J* or *C*, respectively, in place of the *N*. Marine Corps staffs utilize an *S* in a similar nomenclature scheme.

The Administrative Network

The administrative chain of command is concerned with the preparedness of the force. Commander, Fleet Forces Command (CFFC) reports to the secretary of the Navy through the chief of naval operations on the readiness and training of all Navy units. Fleet Forces Command organizes Navy units by type: air, submarine, and surface. The readiness of each is overseen by a type commander (TYCOM). For the surface navy, a type commander—Commander, Naval Surface Forces Atlantic and Pacific—works on each coast. Each TYCOM assigns supervision of individual ships to a squadron or group, known as immediate superiors in the chain of command (ISIC). Serious concerns with manning, training, or equipping the ships are passed from the ship to the ISIC, to the TYCOM, and then on to Fleet Forces Command for resolution. In this respect, the TYCOM and Fleet Forces Command exercise administrative control (ADCON) over ships. Remember that both your warfighting personnel and material readiness start with your ability to fully utilize your ADCON resources.

The Manning Control Authority and the Bureau of Personnel

The administrative chain of command handles manning issues (which will be discussed in more detail in chapter 4). Problems arise when the ship runs short of personnel, particularly if it loses a sailor who holds an important Navy Enlisted Classification (NEC) code. Using established procedures the ship reports the problem to the ISIC and the TYCOM. When necessary, Fleet Forces Command gets involved. As the manning control authority, CFFC sets the desired level of manning readiness for ships for the Bureau of Personnel (specifically PERS-4013), which responds to prioritized manning requests and dispatches orders to sailors. PERS-4013 was formerly known as the Enlisted Placement Management Center (EPMAC).

Afloat Training Group

Training is vital to readiness, and scheduling exercises and schools according to the Surface Forces Training Manual requires a good relationship with the ISIC and Afloat Training Group (ATG). While the ISIC is responsible for certifying ship's training, the type commander requires ATG to observe, evaluate, and make recommendations to the ISIC. The training liaison officer (TLO) is the ship's main point of contact with ATG. A strong relationship with the TLO, to the point of being a member of the Wardroom, will ease tensions in the training cycle. Scheduling and ATG will be discussed in detail in chapter 2, "Planning and Scheduling," and chapter 3, "Training."

Regional Maintenance Centers

Readiness requires that equipment be properly maintained. Port engineers are the ship's advocates to the maintenance community. When ship's crew cannot make repairs or if assistance is required, regional maintenance centers provide the required support. The port engineer and Ops must work hand-in-hand when scheduling maintenance, which is critically important in the life cycle of a ship and a key to material readiness. Regional maintenance centers typically do not have access to classified schedules and therefore require feedback to ensure that the ship has a tailored maintenance schedule that supports training and operation (and not the reverse). Work with the port engineer to schedule quarterly continuous maintenance availabilities. Restricted availability periods, during which a ship is often moved to a dry dock or shipyard for maintenance work, reset the ship's readiness cycle to the maintenance phase and are significant events in a ship's life. Upon completion of this phase the ship will enter the basic phase of the Fleet Response Plan and the crew will begin to train toward the next deployment.

The ship's maintenance and material officer (SMMO) is typically an experienced division officer, warrant officer, or limited duty officer, and the ship's liaison with the port engineer (who works for the type commander) and the maintenance community. A good relationship between Ops and the SMMO will minimize scheduling conflicts and canceled or delayed work caused by mutually exclusive events such as active sonar and hull cleaning.

THE OPERATIONAL CHAIN OF COMMAND

The operations officer must understand and participate in either the strike group or task force professional network (or both) by establishing contact with the various organizations that support, or are supported by, the ship. The first and most important relationship to cultivate is with the immediate superior in the chain of command, or ISIC. Generally, the ISIC is the squadron or group that "owns" your ship and the only element that is in both the operational and administrative chains of command. When possible, spend time with the ISIC prior to reporting to the ship or staff (a meeting that may be included as an intermediate stop on your orders). This time will prove valuable if spent getting to know the staff's key players, its decision-making process, and the boss' expectations.

The Squadron

Ships commanded by a Navy commander (O-5) are assigned to a destroyer squadron (DESRON) or amphibious squadron (PHIBRON). Likewise, patrol coastal ships and mine countermeasures ships are assigned to patrol coastal squadron (PCRON) and mine counter-measure squadron (MCMRON), respectively. Squadron commodores are Navy captains, whose second-tour department heads (also known as N-codes) lead operations (N3), material readiness (N4), and combat systems (N5). During the training phase there will likely be significant interaction between the ship's department heads and the staff's N-codes. Particular attention should be paid to preventing competing requirements from developing, and any schedule discussion must include Ops. Strong communication among the department heads and between the department heads and their staff counterparts is required to prevent unwelcome surprises.

The Strike Group

Ships commanded by a Navy captain (O-6) are directly assigned to carrier strike groups or expeditionary strike groups. Led by an admiral, the carrier strike group includes a destroyer squadron, one or two cruisers, an aircraft carrier, and a carrier air wing, each commanded by a Navy captain. Experience in O-5 level command is a prerequisite for command as an O-6, often referred to as major commands. Also led by an admiral, an expeditionary strike group (when operational) includes an amphibious readiness group, a cruiser, and two or three destroyer-type ships. Each type of strike group includes additional units such as replenishment ships, submarines, and maritime patrol and reconnaissance aircraft.

Given the complexity of operations and scope of assets, the strike group network decentralizes command and control through the composite warfare commander concept, in which a small group of warfare commanders marshals resources in three dimensions and projects power over hundreds of miles. It also relies on "command by negation," a principle that encourages initiative and creativity but allows for the strike group commander to negate, or call off, a subordinate's actions. This aspect of Navy culture contrasts significantly with other military services. Maintaining a strong working relationship with someone on the strike group staff is an effective way to keep your CO informed and to position your ship or squadron as an asset. It is also important to regularly review the strike group's Web site in order to remain current on organization, guidance, schedules, and required reports.

The Numbered Fleet at Home: Second and Third Fleet

Second and Third Fleet are responsible for training and certifying independent ships and strike groups for deployment. Despite their main role as force providers for deployed forces, they also have substantial responsibilities related to homeland defense. Major training and certification events include force protection exercises, Comprehensive Task Unit Exercise (COMPTUEX), and Joint Task Force Exercises (JTFEX). Second and Third Fleet also schedule training events for nonship units such as aviation squadrons and special warfare. The forum utilized to sort out the allocation of services and mutual support is the quarterly fleet scheduling conference. Whether or not the ISIC delegates scheduling functions to the ship, it is worthwhile to attend these conferences if the ship is in port, and advisable if the ship is conducting local operations. No one knows your schedule better than you do, and opportunities may arise for those present to fill important training roles or port visits. Getting to know how units are scheduled, who makes the calls, and what the needs are within the chain of command are all important data points. For example, securing a great port visit might be easier if your ship also schedules duty-related requirements such as deck landing qualifications for helicopter units in their own training cycle. Review the fleet's Operations Order (OPORD) and become familiar with expectations and reporting requirements. As of this writing, Second Fleet's duties have been absorbed by Fleet Forces Command for Atlantic Fleet ships. The "merged functions" of Second Fleet and Fleet Forces Command are now run by Commander, Task Force 20 (CTF 20).

The Numbered Fleet Deployed: Fourth, Fifth, Sixth, and Seventh Fleets

The deployed fleets work for the Navy components of the regional combatant commander (COCOM). Seventh Fleet works for Commander, Pacific Fleet under Pacific

Command (PACOM.) Sixth Fleet works for Commander, Naval Forces Europe and Africa, the Navy component of European Command and Africa Command. At times the fleet commander is also the Navy component commander. For example, under Central Command (CENTCOM), Fifth Fleet is also the Navy component known as U.S. Navy Central (NAVCENT). The same is true for Fourth Fleet, the Navy component of Southern Command.

At the theater level the fleet's network is composed of task force commanders who coordinate fleet actions across the entire geographic area of responsibility. For example, logistics and surveillance in Fifth Fleet are provided by Commander, Task Force 53 and Commander, Task Force 57, respectively. All numbered fleet staffs use the Maritime Operations Center (MOC) concept to varying degrees to run theater-level operations. This is largely transparent to individual ships. A visit to fleet headquarters can clarify the decision-making processes in the theater as well as the requirements the fleet is working to meet. For example, the Theater Security Cooperation Plan (TSCP) is the fleet's plan to work with allies, visit partners, and assert customary law. At the ship level the fleet's OPORD is the most important source document for conducting operations while either deployed or at home.

Ops must be familiar not only with the destination theater, but with any theater that the ship will transit—each of which differs in reporting requirements and available support. The significance of these differences becomes apparent when such details as reporting, logistics support, force protection, and liberty policy are studied.

Some ships are home-ported overseas; others may soon be. These ships are part of the forward deployed naval forces. Assignments to ships home-ported in Yokosuka and Sasebo, Japan, are exciting and rewarding and build considerable operational experience. Rotational crews on mine countermeasures ships and coastal patrol ships deploy to Bahrain; discussions have also been held about expanding the number of forward-deployed ships to include ballistic missile defense platforms.

Other Networks: The Waterfront

Finally, the local network of operations officers in home port is also important to training and readiness. This network includes port operations, local airspace, and training range control as well as sister ships. Understanding port operations helps with everything from routine berthing services to oil spill reporting and response. The local Fleet Area Control and Surveillance Facility (FACSFAC) coordinates the use of airspace and training ranges. At-sea training in the local operations areas (OPAREA) includes live-fire exercises, electronic warfare services, towed targets, aerial target drones, etc., that must be coordinated through FACSFAC and in some cases ATG. Finally, sister ships share port resources, including berthing and pier services, and they can also be important sources of support for training and exercises. Relationships established during previous tours or in department head school can facilitate cooperation.

In summary, the operations officer works simultaneously in two different networks. Within the lifelines Ops is a key cog in the ship's chain of command. Dynamic leadership is required to fully empower ship personnel to perform at the highest level. From this base, Ops can confidently advocate for the ship in the global network of the operational Navy.

PROFESSIONAL TIPS:

Within the lifelines:

- Conduct a department assessment about a month after assuming your duties. In a memo or e-mail to the CO, briefly summarize your long-range goals, plans, and focus of effort.

- Find a mechanism for establishing priorities and gathering input such as a brief meeting of *just* department heads over coffee.

- Build with the departmental LCPO a creative and mutually beneficial relationship that includes regular meetings and walks through departmental berthing areas.

- Check with senior LDOs or the LDO detailer before writing fitness reports for your Ops LDO.

- A strong correlation exists between program effectiveness and chiefs being out "on the deck-plates." Lead by example and make your expectations in this regard known.

- Challenge the first class petty officers to run the daily routine starting with muster, instruction, and inspection. Meet quarterly with the first class petty officers and the departmental LCPO.

Outside the lifelines:
- Be familiar with the Enlisted Distribution Verification Record and the rating assignment officers relevant to the operations department. See chapter 4.

- Maintain a good working relationship with the project manager, mission coordinator, training liaison officer, and scheduler at Afloat Training Group. See chapter 3.

- Talk regularly with the port engineer regarding the ship's schedule. Both the port engineer and the operations officer are essential participants in each PBFT.

- When possible, spend time with the ISIC prior to reporting to the ship or staff. This may be included in your orders as an intermediate stop.

- Be familiar with the strike group's Web site.

  - Pay particular attention to the strike group's "battle rhythm," the daily process of meetings and briefs, for direction and coordination of daily and future operations.

- For more on command and control, read Naval Doctrine Publication 6, Naval Command and Control.

- For more on the composite warfare concept, read Naval Warfare Publication 3-56, Composite Warfare Commander's Manual.

- Read the numbered fleet's General Operational Guidance (OPGEN) and standing operations order (OPORDER) for each area of operations.

  - Specifically, understand fleet guidance for minimum fuel requirements, ready for sea (RFS) status, disabled machinery requests, excess speed of advance (XSOA), and port operations overtime; and ready duty ship assignments and requirements.

- Read the local port's administrative instruction (SOPA Admin).

- Read the local FACSFAC instruction for instructions on requesting services and checking in and out of ranges.

CHAPTER 2

PLANNING AND SCHEDULING

BLUF:

- *Effective personal organization is essential for skilled management of the department.*
- *Plans must be methodically constructed but adaptable for execution.*

RDML J. D. KELLY, CTF 70, SITS AT THE COMMANDER'S CHAIR ABOARD USS CHANCELLORSVILLE DURING A COMBINED EXERCISE WITH THE JAPANESE MARITIME SELF-DEFENSE FORCE, 2004.

Author's collection.

A BLY OR POORLY, officers are always leading. Numerous methodologies for teaching leaders exist, but it seems that leadership is more art than science. Management skills, however, can be taught. More importantly, skilled management enables leadership by exemplifying solid organization, utilizing professional knowledge, and, most significantly, making time to devote to leading. Planning and scheduling are management functions that the operations officer must master and pass on to division officers.

PREPARATION

New operations officers are immediately ordered to attend the Surface Warfare Officers School department head course. Most surface warriors reach this point with about seven-and-a-half years of commissioned service. The diverse experience gained during those initial years may nevertheless include only a single ship tour. Follow-on shore duty assignments, particularly in training commands and higher headquarters, can contribute to a better understanding of fleet and force responsibilities and goals. Regardless of experience, the curricula for the operations officer specialty section and the department head course focus clearly on the tasks ahead. The department head course offers time to study important documents, ask questions, discuss the material, and work on collateral duty management (discussed in more detail in chapter 8), as well as the opportunity to begin building professional networks with fellow department heads, as discussed in chapter 1.

PERSONAL ORGANIZATION

The operations officer must be well-organized and able to handle large volumes of information, including the department's workload, tasks from the ISIC and TYCOM, and the ship's short-, medium-, and long-term schedules. In addition to managing the department on board, the operations officer spends considerable time responding to communications from outside the ship. In the past, Navy officers depended on "wheel books"—pocket-sized, spiral-bound notebooks—to help keep their affairs in order. The Navy as an organization, meanwhile, has traditionally communicated from higher headquarters and between individual ships and units through "message traffic," which evolved from flag signals in the days of sail to radio transmissions in the industrial age. Ops reviewed incoming messages and forwarded them to the captain. (If the message was of general interest, it was posted on a "read board.") Now, as then, the operations officer is responsible for reading all the messages pertaining to the ship (incoming and outgoing). Reading and reviewing message traffic takes time and should not detract from other responsibilities, including standing watch.

In today's increasingly complex world, wheel books and read boards are, for the operations officer, no longer sophisticated enough. Message traffic is now delivered electronically through e-mail. E-mail programs such as Microsoft Outlook can be tailored to suit personal taste and used to prioritize and track messages and assignments, delegation, and due dates. Whatever system the operations officer devises must be understood and accessible by subordinates. E-mail represents a large percentage of the department's dynamic workload. Consider it all official correspondence and respond to it professionally. Be specific in delegation and prioritization, and follow assignments to completion—including acknowledgment by whoever assigned the task (all of which can be automated in the Outlook program). Your reputation, and by extension, that of your ship, is largely based on timely and well-reasoned correspondence.

The department's routine workload—including maintenance, required briefings, training assignments, etc.—is typically known far in advance. Forehanded planning is the critical element in managing this part of your department. Your sailors must have time to complete this work, and your leadership must supervise it. As Ops, you will need to expend time and effort to get acquainted with everything from boat and lifejacket maintenance to computer backups and monthly communications security management. This will require solid planning and efficient delegation of responsibility.

THE LONG-RANGE SCHEDULE

The first step in drafting a long-range schedule for the ship is determining where she sits in the Fleet Response Plan (FRP) cycle. Known as an employment cycle, a ship's life span consists of four phases: maintenance, basic, integrated, and sustainment. The time period actually spent in maintenance is called "maintenance availability." Continuous maintenance availability (CMAV) lasts from two to six weeks and is scheduled throughout the Fleet Response Plan cycle. In contrast, chief of naval operations–sponsored availability (CNO availability) lasts from two to six months for a surface ship and constitutes the FRP's maintenance phase.

When the ship is materially ready and completes the maintenance phase, the crew begins training in the basic phase, working toward certification with the support of the ISIC and ATG over a twenty-week period. Once certified, the ship enters the integrated training phase in which ships train together as a strike group. Finally, the ship reaches the sustainment phase, which includes deployment and whatever time remains before the next maintenance phase. In the past this cycle was nominally a two-year process. The current FRP, however, is designed to lengthen the sustainment phase and increase the ship's availability for tasking.

THE FLEET RESPONSE PLAN

The FRP is a framework for providing Navy forces around the globe. As described in Chief of Naval Operations Instruction 5000.15, it is designed to deploy Navy ships on a rotating basis to the various fleet areas of responsibility. The goal is to provide forward presence based on a defined force requirement, also known as Global Force Management. The FRP also requires forces to be available to surge forward when not deployed, responding on short notice to world events.

Ships are trained and certified in defined, progressive levels of employable and deployable capability. An FRP cycle runs from the end of one maintenance phase to the end of the next. For surface combatants, this means 27–32 months. The FRP maintenance phase ensures that the material condition of the ship supports appropriate readiness throughout the rest of the FRP cycle. Personnel processes within the FRP maintain appropriate unit manning levels throughout the entire readiness cycle. Training within the FRP provides required levels of mission readiness early in the training cycle and sustains targeted readiness levels throughout the FRP phases.

The FRP certifies ships for mission assignments based on the particular phase the ship is in. Major shipyard or depot-level repairs, upgrades, and modernization installations are scheduled during the maintenance phase. For surface ships, this is a transitional period marked by personnel turnover as well as industrial repairs and other upgrades. Crews are expected to use the in-port time to their advantage, for classes, team trainers, and other opportunities. The latest Surface Forces Training Manual guidance also requires continuous certification in damage control, force protection, maintenance and material management (3-M), supply, and medical training throughout the maintenance phase.

Following this phase, the ship begins unit-level training (ULT) in the basic phase, focusing on warfare-area certifications as defined in the SFTM. Guided by the ATG and the ship's ISIC and supported by the Center for Surface Combat Systems Detachments, ULT includes team training both on board and ashore; unit-level exercises in port and at sea; and unit inspections, assessments, qualifications, and certifications. Additionally, units maximize in-port synthetic training options for individual teams as well as the entire unit. Units that complete the basic phase are certified as independent units ready for tasking (RFT) or capable of amphibious task force surge. RFT ships may be tasked with independent operations in support of Shaping or Deterrence, Defense Support to Civil Authority, Humanitarian Assistance/Disaster Relief, or other specific, focused operations. Others may be employed in support of homeland defense; counter-narcotics operations; visit, board, search and seizure missions; or other, similarly focused missions. Amphibious task force surge applies only to amphibious assault ships; it does not imply Marine Corps capability because the ships in the task force do not integrate with the Marine air-ground task force. Those ships designated as amphibious task force surge capable may support special operations forces, special purpose Marine air-ground task forces, and adaptive force packages, or provide lift as required.

Ships that complete the basic phase are ready to work in coordinated strike groups (or other combined-arms forces) in a multidimensional warfare environment in the integrated phase. This phase provides an opportunity for decision-makers and watchstanders to complete staff planning and warfare commander's courses; conduct multi-unit, in-port and at-sea training; and build on individual and unit skills. The purpose of the integrated phase is to certify ships to meet the combatant commander's (COCOM) request for specific capabilities—such as those gained during maritime security surge (MSS) or major combat operations. MSS training ensures proficiency in conducting surge missions, and includes live training that emphasizes multi-unit procedures and anticipated, region-specific scenarios such as maritime interception operations, expanded maritime interception operations, Strategic Offensive Forces support, antipiracy operations, theater security cooperation, and information operations. Certifications for a second type of surge capability, major combat operations (MCO) surge, include proficiency in intelligence, surveillance, and reconnaissance, command and control, air operations, maritime operations, information operations, power projection, ballistic missile defense, peacetime presence, amphibious operations, special operations forces support, combat search and rescue, mine warfare, sustainment and stability operations, and Anti-terrorism/Force Protection (AT/FP). These units will have demonstrated the capability to function as a naval combat force, but not necessarily to lead such operations.

A unit or group attains "MCO Ready" status through advanced integrated training and by demonstrating the ability to lead joint or coalition operations, not simply by participating in them, as is the case with MCO surge missions. Upon completion of integrated training the unit is certified as fully capable of conducting all forward-deployed operations. During deployment, units and forces maintain proficiency through ongoing training, exercises, and normal operations, as directed by higher authority.

The sustainment phase begins upon completion of the integrated phase, continues throughout the post-deployment period, and ends with the commencement of the maintenance phase. During post-deployment sustainment, training events will be scheduled and conducted as necessary to maintain appropriate readiness for MCO. Sustainment phase training drills aggregated units and staffs in complex, multi-mission planning and execution and how to operate in a joint or coalition environment. Sustainment training, in port and at sea, allows forces to demonstrate proficiency in operating as part of a joint or coalition combined force, and ensures continued MCO readiness. The extent of sustainment training will vary depending on how long the unit has maintained MCO Ready status and on that force's anticipated tasking. Deployments in support of the Combatant Commanders' Global Force Management requirements may occur during the sustainment phase after numbered fleet commanders recertify groups and units.

FLEET EMPLOYMENT SCHEDULES

The numbered fleet commander maintains the official ship's schedule. The fleet schedulers maintain a list of events and other needs ranging from port visits to training evolutions. Using historical data, they project these requirements well out into the future. Port visits, particularly highly desired appearances at Fleet Week in New York or the Portland Rose Festival, are sometimes planned a year in advance based on a ship's projected phase (maintenance phase, basic phase, etc.). Fleet scheduling conferences are typically held on a quarterly basis, and include the participation of operations officers from major commands. Ships with more junior commanders may not directly participate in negotiations at these conferences, but because a good deal of scheduling information is available, attendance is highly recommended. ISICs are usually required to concur with proposed schedules for the coming quarter and brief any issues that affect their implementation. Negotiations over future quarters may also take place here. Deals may include placeholders or "penciling in" a ship for later tasking pending further coordination.

The Web-based program used to manage ship schedule information is called "Websked," which depicts the ship's schedule on a bar graph with notations for each specific ship employment. Your ISIC must approve a tentative schedule before it is submitted to the fleet schedulers for final endorsement. Ship schedules are classified as confidential; approved schedules can be found on the classified network. Keep your personal copy of the schedule up to date with the status of proposed changes and clearly differentiate between what is approved and what is pending.

AN EXECUTIVE SCHEDULE

A simple executive overview of the ship's schedule for the CO and XO should include key dates of significant milestones in the ship's life cycle. Aside from commissioning and decommissioning, the three biggest happenings in a ship's life cycle are deployments, CNO maintenance availability periods, and inspections by the Board of Inspection and Survey (INSURV). The strike group and ISIC will typically provide the ship with important pre-deployment dates. Chapter 3 of the Joint Fleet Maintenance Manual, Volume II, details important planning milestones for CNO availability in Appendix A. Finally, INSURV and the TYCOM both provide significant guidance on preparing for INSURV, including long-range plans of action and milestones, on their Web sites. Collating these three sets of milestones in a long-range calendar provides a quick visual reference and executive requirements for the ship's leaders.

Another executive schedule format might include key dates in the ship's employment cycle for readiness. Through the Defense Readiness Reporting System for the Navy (DRRS-N), ship's readiness is measured in five "pillars": personnel, equipment, supply, training, and ordnance. Personnel reporting requirements are based on deployment dates; the Personnel Manning Report (PERSMAR) is required periodically from one year prior to deployment. The equipment pillar is based on a maintenance figure of merit and, from a long-range perspective, the ship's plan for chief of naval operations–sponsored CMAV should be included. Supply milestones include annual inventories and inspections leading to certification. The training pillar is derived from TORIS/TFOM; milestones associated with it include basic phase certifications, intermediate and advanced training, and exercises. Finally, the ordnance pillar is centered on ammunition off- and on-load dates and explosives safety certifications. More detailed than the first executive plan, this plan covers much of the same information. Its advantage lies in its direct correlation to DRRS-N readiness reporting. Either of these formats (or a combination of both) can be summarized briefly using Microsoft Excel.

A Working Schedule

The operations officer works each day from a Websked-based schedule (in an Excel spreadsheet) that should include notes from meetings, e-mail, and phone calls that may affect it. It should also include backup plans, particularly when weather or outside services are involved. A common complaint by ship's company is, "The schedule always changes and I can't plan ahead." The same off-ship forces—fleet requirements, emergent maintenance, cascading effects of other operations, and other disruptions—affect the set schedules of all U.S. Navy ships. Those ships with flexible, well-planned schedules and clear communication between the CO, Ops, and the crew tend to avoid schedule-related morale problems.

Schedule changes are sometimes unavoidable, as when a supporting element in a multi-unit event is delayed or withdraws from participation. Resolving such an issue requires tasking a ship that was scheduled for other duty. Responsible schedulers need both up-to-date schedule information and accurate estimates of equipment casualty repair. Frequent communication with the appropriate network offers the best chance for a workable backup plan, the time to arrange alternative coverage, or at least a warning of impending change.

SCHEDULING FOR CONTINGENCIES

An effective working schedule allows for contingencies. Joint Pub 5-0 defines a contingency as a "situation requiring military operations in response to natural disasters, terrorists, subversives, or as otherwise directed by appropriate authority to protect US interests." Contingencies are handled with a combination of pre-planned responses and crisis action planning. Fleet commanders often review unit schedules and, as part of a pre-planned response, designate certain assets to be available. For example, ships in Second and Third Fleets are assigned as duty ships to support pre-planned responses to contingencies such as defense support to civil authorities and maritime homeland defense. Such assignments require heightened, ready-for-sea requirements (being prepared to sail within twenty-four hours, for example). A prudent operations officer will notify outside units that will be affected by the ship's new assignment, and draw up a backup plan. It is also important to have a go-to training schedule in order to take advantage of situations in which contingency duty is not needed. Ops should maintain a list of SFTM-based training requirements and prepared briefs ready to be implemented if the opportunity arises. This is a great task to delegate to the training officer.

Operations and Planning

Translating the working schedule and the detailed schedule produced at PBFT into a schedule of events for sea is covered in chapter 5.

Navy Planning

Planning at the unit level is really about schedules. At the squadron, strike group, and numbered fleet commander level, planning is geared around accomplishing a mission for the fleet or higher headquarters. Examples of missions that follow the planning process include tactical operations such as choke-point transits, noncombatant evacuations, and even bilateral exercises (though, due to deployment time-lines, much of the planning for these may not include the participating unit). The planning process is taught in Joint Professional Military Education courses and schools such as the Joint Maritime Tactics Course. As an operations officer you may be called to participate in planning sessions for theater-level operations, operations plans (war plans), or at strike group warfare commander's conferences.

Planning for each service follows a particular (but similar) process that includes mission analysis, course of action development, comparison and decision, and orders development—all of which conform to Joint Publication 5-0, *Joint Operation Planning.* Naval Warfare Publication 5-01, *Navy Planning,* is the key document for the Navy planning process, and offers a systematic approach for analyzing the operational environment and building a coherent framework for decisions. If you are scheduled to participate in a planning conference with Marines, first review Marine Corps Doctrine Publication 5, *Planning*. When working with Special Operations Capable Marines, you may be involved in the Rapid Response Planning Process (R2P2). Marine Corps Working Paper 5-1, *Marine Corps Planning Process*, Appendix J, is entitled "Rapid Planning" and covers R2P2.

At first, the full Navy planning process may seem cumbersome and time-consuming. Training and frequent use of it will build proficiency. The process is designed to systematically analyze the mission; develop war game courses of action (COAs) against projected enemy courses of action (ECOAs); select a COA; and produce a military decision in the form of a directive such as an operation plan (OPLAN) or OPORD. NWP 5-01 emphasizes that while the time available to plan may change, the process does not. To be ready for those instances when preparation time is limited, experienced planners will practice crisis action planning (see NWP 5-01 Appendix M).

Plans of Action and Milestones

An extremely useful tool for planning a specific event, such as a change of command or an upcoming inspection, is a document known as the plan of action and milestones (POAM, "PO-AM" or "P-O-A-and-M"). Working backwards from the date of the event, the planner can tie required action to specific dates (milestones) and assign responsibilities to particular crew members. The keys to success are tying milestones to actual dates on the calendar (avoiding holidays and conflicting events) and holding people accountable through meetings and follow-through. POAMs can help the ship recover from a substandard inspection or spot-check; they demonstrate that required corrective actions are identified and can be executed. They are also useful in tracking eligibility for ship awards over an extended period of time. Ops can build regular progress reviews into the plan and manage conflicts with a long-term goal in mind. POAMs and reverse planning are useful management techniques that will be covered again in chapter 8.

Professional Tips:

- Spend your time at SWOs wisely by reading tactical and technical publications and theater-related documents, and preparing collateral duties. It will be too late for such preparations once you are on the job.

- Plan to respond to naval messages seventy-two hours prior to the required due date in order to provide your chain of command with enough time to review the references and the proposed response.

- An 80 percent solution delivered on time is better than a 100 percent solution that is overcome by events ("O-B-E") while being fine-tuned.

- A great reference for operations officers and aspiring surface warriors to study is Allied Tactical Publication 1 (ATP-1), *Maritime Tactical Instructions and Procedures,* Volume I. It covers command and control and many of the missions that ships perform. Surface Warfare Officers are generally familiar with Volume II, the tactical signals portion.

- Ops is responsible for reading all message traffic pertaining to the ship.

- Utilize Outlook e-mail and task functions to their maximum capability.

- Provide the CO, XO, SEL, and other department heads with an executive plan.

CHAPTER 3

TRAINING:
LEADERSHIP AND MANAGEMENT

BLUF:

- *Training prepares the crew for a mission.*
- *Readiness reflects the crew's ability to perform the mission with available personnel, equipment, supply, training, and ordnance.*

MCM Crew DOMINANT personnel stream sweep gear aboard USS SCOUT in the Arabian Gulf, 2007.

Author's collection.

PART I: TRAINING PHILOSOPHY

THE NAVY PROVIDES THE NATION with the capability to conduct prompt and sustained combat operations at sea. The spectrum of its missions—from presence and deterrence to humanitarian response—is vested in the unique nature of naval combat capability. The Navy's non-combat missions are inherent, if subordinate, to its combat mission. To provide the nation with capabilities ranging from pier sentry duty to major combat operations, the Navy mans, trains, and equips "warships, ready for tasking." Training for missions is conducted on the individual sailor and unit level with increasing complexity through multidimensional, joint, and combined task force exercises.

The reality of today's terrorist threat and overseas engagements requires ships to be ready at all times. The Navy, therefore, seeks to maximize such preparedness. Prior to issuance of the Fleet Response Plan construct discussed in chapter 2, the reduced, post-deployment readiness of ships (due to personnel turnover and a lengthy maintenance period) had a broad "bathtub" effect (measured graphically, this drop in readiness reflected the outline of a bathtub) on the Navy. And while no ship can be ready 100 percent of the time, the Navy is testing a new approach to improve both training and material readiness. The current training policy is spelled out in the Surface Force Training Manual (SFTM, or "Sur-For-Tray-Man"). The "pilot program" being tested is designed to simplify training requirements and deal realistically with current manning and maintenance issues. It focuses specifically on the type commander's responsibilities: training in the maintenance and basic phases. During the integrated and sustainment phases, the numbered fleet commander manages training.

The Current Approach to Training

The Surface Force Training Manual is the Navy's primary source of training policy, direction and requirements. It focuses on certifications for each warfare area and provides guidance for maintaining continuous readiness and certification throughout the Fleet Response Plan by requiring specific readiness metrics during each phase. Certifications are assessed according to a Training Figure of Merit (TFOM)— a score based on the ship's assessment of its proficiency and tracking of training events. This score is obtained using the Training and Operational Information Services (TORIS).

On a computer screen, these tools produce a stoplight, or digital dashboard format for briefing, with red, yellow, blue, or green colors indicating a level of proficiency supported by data. Ideally, these indicators are used to tailor training and resources to a specific unit's needs. The SFTM is fundamentally designed to assist ship's training teams in effectively assessing and improving the crew's proficiency and securing the ship's certification in required mission areas during the basic phase. Once this is accomplished the ship is considered "ready for tasking," if not yet proficient in group or other composite unit operations. As the crew continues training throughout the integrated and sustainment phases, Continuous Certification Requirements (CCRs) are tracked to ensure proficiency.

This is a broad-brush description of a complex and intricate system. The operations officer and training officer must work hand-in-hand to plan, execute, document, and track each requirement within each mission area. Additionally, many CCRs include a ninety-day rolling window requiring both repetition and re-validation that cannot expire. A great way to gain knowledge and experience with TORIS/TFOM and CCRs is to assign junior officers as warfare leads in each mission area. The warfare leads are responsible for the planning, execution, and documentation of all training in their respective areas. A thorough study of the SFTM while in department head school is strongly recommended in order to effectively manage the warfare leads.

The Surface Force Readiness "Pilot" Program

Where the SFTM concentrates on "training the trainers," the pilot program seeks to educate the crew with more than training alone. The pilot training strategy begins with a material assessment, on the assumption that material condition must support training before training can be effective. Following this assessment, the ATG conducts training in theory and fundamentals, and then offers practical, hands-on scenarios with "over-the-shoulder" training. Only then is the crew rated on its ability to accomplish a mission. Lastly, an inspection ensures that standards and proficiency are being maintained.

One seismic difference between the SFTM and the pilot program is that in the latter, the ship must meet minimum equipment standards prior to moving from the maintenance phase into the training phase. Progression from one FTRP phase to the next will not include "social promotions" based on the calendar. The ship must demonstrate to a third party proficiency and a material condition that supports training. Aiming to eventually have watch teams train each other, ATG will provide training teams during the basic phase, allowing the crew to maintain proficiency during the subsequent integrated and sustainment phases. This approach also lets the crew focus on mission execution instead of scenario development during the basic phase, which in turn allows it to "maximize the number of crewmembers that receive training on the watch position they will be assigned on deployment."[1] The pilot program also directly addresses the DRRS-N pillars of personnel, equipment, supply, training, and ordnance. Under it, the training pillar still utilizes a Training Figure of Merit (TFOM). But it is a simpler process than under the

---

1 From unpublished draft of Training Pilot Manual, section 102-4.c, 1-2, Dated February 10, 2011.

SFTM, with straightforward grading and fewer exercises required less frequently.

The pilot program offers tiered progression from the maintenance phase through the basic phase. Progress is based on exit criteria defined for each PESTO pillar, and required to be met before beginning the next tier. During Tier 0, in which crew members are expected to attend critical schools, material readiness is the focus. Tier 1, the mobility tier, features training in core skills such as engineering, navigation, seamanship, damage control, etc. To complete Tier 1, crew members must safely operate the ship, navigate, and communicate. Tier 2 includes unit tactical training in air warfare, ballistic missile defense, surface warfare, undersea warfare, etc. Completing this tier requires successfully maneuvering and tactically employing the ship's weapons and sensors. In Tier 3, the ship integrates with other units into multi-platform and multiple warfare areas with the goal of operating with a strike group or other, high-level organization, while alternating between duty as a Search and Attack Unit Commander (SAUC), Surface Action Group Commander (SAGC), and Warfare Area Commander or Coordinator. In other words, the ship's crew will develop the skills required for deployment and, possibly, major combat operations. Tier 4 is the sustainment phase, by which point the ship is expected to be proficient in each warfare area.

Again, this is broad overview of a new, experimental program; the draft manual contains more specific details. Currently, the inaugural class of pilot program ships is testing its efficacy.

PART II: TRAINING MANAGEMENT

The Training Officer

First formalized in the surface fleet during the 1990s as part of the "Smart Ship" concept, the training officer (TRAINO) position was developed to provide the commanding officer greater visibility into sailors' training and a ship's embedded systems. The TRAINO position has expanded to include the network of training options available in the ship's home port and beyond.

The most recent SFTM formalized TRAINO's duties, which are the nexus of training "between the lifelines" as well as outside them. The training officer supervises the sailors' Personnel Qualifications Standard (PQS) program; maintains the formal school requirements program and coordinates school quotas; tracks Navy Enlisted Classification (NEC) codes and schools completion; trains the crew on Navy Knowledge On-line (NKO), eLearning, and electronic training jackets; works with Fleet Training Management and Planning Systems (FLTMPS); and ensures that Relational Admin (RADM) is up to date. Beyond the lifelines, TRAINO maintains the TORIS database; provides the CO with assessments of mission readiness using TORIS, TFOM, and CCRs; attends TRAINO and school coordinator meetings; maintains access to the ATG Web site; and coordinates with Ops in scheduling training exercises. The most effective training officers are integral to PBFT, defending the needs of individual sailors and prioritizing off-ship training. Many also run their ship's Division in the Spotlight Program. Change 1 to the SFTM provides a useful TRAINO "tickler" as a checklist of recurring duties.

Organizing the Training Program

For administrative purposes, shipboard training easily breaks down by warfare areas, which feature separate proficiency requirements met on weekly, monthly, quarterly, or annual bases. Someone from each warfare area should advocate for training time. Ops must organize and prioritize competing requirements and plan for optimal success. Often left out of warfare area planning is the need to address non-warfare training, including advancement, general military training, requirements for safety programs, etc. Advocates for these requirements are needed to ensure a well-rounded and executable schedule that can be planned and posted in advance. Typical but sometimes neglected products of the planning process include watch team replacement plans, long- and short-range training plans, and a two-week calendar during the PBFT.

Scheduling Training

On a calendar, federal holidays should be blocked out first. During the basic phase much of the schedule is driven by services or training team availability. The operations officer must also deal with schedule changes forced by fleet requirements. Beyond the basic phase, a good training plan will prepare the ship for deployment and keep required training proficiencies current.

Ops should have access to the schedules of other ships in the squadron, local replenishment schedules, available services, and schools in order to exploit every training opportunity. Last-minute changes in schedules or attendance levels may enable Ops to send a sailor to a school with a vacancy. Additionally, opportunities to cross-deck an officer or even a team to another ship that offers a special evolution should not go unnoticed. Awareness of the ship's needs and waterfront schedules can pay large dividends.

A structured approach to both in-port and at-sea training will keep the ship's priorities clear to the crew. One such approach is a notional "Warfare Week," although this tack is applicable only outside the basic phase. Monday is always a seamanship training day. Tuesday is combat systems (at sea) and force protection (in port). Wednesday is allotted to damage control and medical; Thursday to engineering; and Friday to integrated training. The goal of this construct is to make training habitual.

Officer Training

Officer training is vital to building a strong wardroom and watch teams. Ideally led by the commanding officer, active department heads or even a group of well-organized and motivated second-tour division officers can provide a solid foundation for surface warfare officer qualification. The key to effective qualification is giving crew members opportunities to actually drive the ship. Commander, Naval Surface Forces recently introduced a Surface Warfare Officer Proficiency book, called the "SWO pro book," to track experience-based training as a means to refresh perishable skills such as conning alongside an oiler or completing pier landings. It will also track ship handling simulator time dating from commissioning.

Division officers report from their commissioning source directly to the fleet, and each ship handles their training differently. The SORN provides the construct of a "junior division officer" that many commands adopt in form, if not in name. Others train them as a group before assigning them to division officer roles. The ship's phase in the FRP also affects possible implementation of a junior officer training plan.

Particular attention should be paid to the underway watchbill for junior officers to ensure that each is afforded opportunities to conduct basic evolutions such as conning in and out of port and approaching a replenishment ship. A fair rotation through all watch stations, including CIC, after-steering, helm safety, etc., builds camaraderie. And setting a high standard for qualification in these foundational watch stations builds confidence and competence for more senior watches.

The training of junior officers should go beyond computer-based classes and Power Point lectures. The tried-and-true method of standing watch under instruction (U/I, or "you-eye") can be freshened by assigning relatively senior officers to stand the watch as instructors and provide perspective and experience beyond that of a division officer. These officers should utilize short (no longer than thirty minutes) "chalk talks" to cover limited topics or upcoming evolutions. Such attention-grabbing chats help bring new watchstanders up to speed on evolutions that are routine to others. Another dynamic training event, a version of "school ship," combines several approaches. A multidisciplinary session, school ship is designed to cover a complex system or concept with a combination of lectures, discussions, and hands-on interaction. Training might begin with a thirty-minute, Operational Tasking (OPTASK) brief and a thirty-minute, system walk-through. A Battle Force Team Trainer (BFTT) scenario might follow, before a discussion of battle orders, standing orders, etc. Other effective but more structured training methods include watchstander "shadowing" in which an individual sailor follows a junior watchstander (of sounding and security for example) for space and equipment familiarization. Skill walk-throughs and demonstrations allow the sailor to show proficiency in tasks such as donning emergency escape breathing devices, emergency egress, operating eductors, close-in weapons system, weapons posture transitions, taking a visual fix, hose handling, line handling, etc.

Don't forget to include traditional methods such as seminar presentation with academic-style discussions; field trips to other ships and squadrons, etc.; evening study (thirty minutes of lecture and walkabout); small-group, leadership discussions with mentors about case studies or current ship issues (prepare for with read-aheads), ship handling, or tactics seminars on battle orders, standing orders, tac-memos, etc.; and old-school lectures and tests in classroom-like settings, a must for Rules of the Road training. None of these training methods are likely to be new to the reader. The point is to consciously utilize them within a structured plan to provide dynamic, interactive training.

Training for the Fight

Ships with embedded training devices such as BFTT boast a tremendous tool for advancing qualifications. Running tactical scenarios in port is an excellent way to offer training opportunities at little risk to equipment or reputation. The ship's Warfare Coordinators—the Surface, Air, and Antisubmarine Warfare Coordinators—should do their best to attend schools and sit in on as many in-port scenarios as possible. For recently reported department heads, a regimen of challenging scenarios can test their SWO training to assure speedy qualification or requalification as Tactical Action Officers (TAO). In addition to tactical efficiency, this post requires a grasp of theater geopolitical sensitivities, intelligence requirements, and operational law on par with that of the operations officer.

Second-tour department heads often work for warfare commanders, and all need to prepare to assume the responsibilities of alternate warfare commanders. Force TAO and force warfare coordinator duties should be practiced to the extent possible prior to assuming them at sea. Appendix A offers a sample Force TAO that suggests the high expectations of this watch in today's demanding geopolitical environment. During the integrated phase, seek out alternate warfare commander duties and take every opportunity to practice with the required watch teams. At a minimum, this will provide insight into the expectations of a warfare commander, whose duties you will likely assume as a second-tour department head.

COMMAND QUALIFICATION

If you aspire to command, start on the qualification process early in your department head tour. If you are not the senior watch officer (SWO), work through the SWO to schedule the required ship-handling evolutions so you can be observed. Press your CO for opportunities to discuss the Command Qualification Board, and to schedule you for one toward the end of your first tour.

PROFESSIONAL TIPS:

- While in Department Head School, study the SFTM in detail.

- Assigning warfare leads to manage SFTM requirements is a proven method of tracking and coordinating them.

- Ensure that TRAINO is using the training officer tickler from the SFTM.

- Schedule around federal holidays to avoid overtime costs.

- Warfare Week is a useful scheduling construct outside the basic phase of training.

- Keep officer training dynamic, hands-on, and interactive.

- Be familiar with Surface Warfare Officer Qualification and Designation, Commander, Naval Surface Force Instruction 1412.1C, dated April 11, 2011.

- Surface warfare officers can now track their navigation, seamanship, and ship-handling proficiency in the "SWO Pro Book," an online resource governed by Commander, Naval Surface Force Instruction 1412.3, dated May 10, 2011.

- If you aspire to command, read the Command Qualification Instruction: Commander, Naval Surface Force Instruction 1412.2, dated May 12, 2010.

CHAPTER 4

MANAGEMENT PART I:
RUNNING THE OPERATIONS DEPARTMENT

BLUF:

■ *An efficient department routine will allow the operations officer to focus attention on planning in port and the schedule of events at sea.*

Deck Division Personnel with USS CHANCELLORSVILLE in dry dock, Yokosuka, Japan, 2004.
Author's collection.

OPERATIONS DEPARTMENTS THROUGHOUT THE FLEET are organized according to ship's bill. Most include a deck, a combat information center (CIC), and an electronic warfare and perhaps a cryptology division. These departments often also feature an enlisted intelligence assistant, a training officer, and an operations limited-duty officer. A clear chain of command, particularly in CIC, is essential to job satisfaction for all involved. Standard Organization and Regulations of the U.S. Navy (SORN) provides useful ideas for assignments, including junior division officers.

DECK DIVISION

Three key elements for success in the deck division are material, training, and safety. A ship's exterior appearance reflects the effectiveness of its command. The operations officer should review the ship's boats and topside preservation and the smartness of her lines daily. Inside the ship, good stowage practices are essential to maintenance and cleanliness. If the senior boatswain's mate is not setting a high standard in this regard, Ops should do so.

A ship's reputation is underpinned by how she looks, and a thorough and proactive topside preservation plan will distinguish your ship from the rest. To establish one, first develop a methodical, long-range plan that covers the whole ship. Two ways of approaching topside preservation are dedicating a small, roving gang to such work, and dividing the ship into zones with a petty officer to oversee the work in each. Both are effective if managed well.

In addition, Ops should push to develop good preservation habits. For example, freshwater wash-down should be completed prior to every return to port. Include hard-to-reach areas such as antenna platforms the day before, if necessary. And whenever possible, protect gun mounts, windlasses, etc., from salt spray with Herculite covers. As with everything, solid preparation prevents poor performance, so review the references and ensure that crew members are using necessary protective equipment, such as respirators. Review the ship's respiratory protection program when you report; surgical masks are not respirators.

The TYCOM is also funding two programs to assist the deck division. Under one, the Corrosion Control Assist Team (CCAT) addresses topside preservation. Under a second, the Deck Maintenance Assist Team (DMAT) provides technical assistance from the regional maintenance center for maintenance of davits, anchor windlasses, boats, etc. Ops should work with the TYCOM to schedule visits from these teams during maintenance availability periods, when the ship can focus on them. Working with CCAT and DMAT are excellent opportunities for junior personnel to learn proper operation and maintenance of deck equipment from technical experts.

Often complex and dangerous, deck evolutions require significant training. Whether operating the ship's boat, lowering the search-and-rescue swimmer into the water, or conducting flight operations, sailors can be placed at unnecessary risk through complacency or poor training. Ops should not only be involved in the execution of these evolutions, but more importantly in ensuring adequate training and qualifications programs.

Effective supervision during deck evolutions requires detailed knowledge of a ship's systems. However, even a novice observer can be effective if he or she asks the right questions. And the Navy's Safety Manual (OPNAVINST 5100.19 series) provides checklists for many of these operations. For safety reasons, it is best to make sure that the division officer and division chief review the checklists during briefs and again during the evolution.

COMBAT INFORMATION CENTER (CIC)

Run by operation specialists (OSs) whose sole duty is watchstanding, CIC is the command center of the ship from which its weapons and combat systems are operated. A second, equally important function of CIC is to provide forceful backup, using all of the ship's sensors, to the bridge to ensure the vessel's safe navigation. Disciplined watchstanding and professional competence are therefore essential for the ship's safety, particularly during special details. And a stringent training and qualification program is necessary for the shipping officer and navigation plotters utilized at sea and anchor detail.

Operations specialists must also be good administrators. The Navy warfare publications custodian, secret control clerk (see Appendix B), and other administrators train junior petty officers to orchestrate the production of daily messages and briefs that drive the ship's battle rhythm. An in-depth knowledge of systems enables junior petty officers to participate in the communications plan, and prepares them for standing tactical data-link coordinator (TDC) and air-control watches as air intercept controller (AIC), antisubmarine tactical air controller (ASTAC), etc.

The watch organization of CIC varies widely between ship classes. Capabilities, casualty control, training, and manning depend on ship doctrine. However, operations specialists on every ship should be experts in readiness reporting and message traffic, proper voice communications and PROWORDS, and radar navigation and piloting. They are normally the voice of a ship, and a strong indicator of its professionalism. Junior OSs well-trained in these everyday tasks will become more capable and sophisticated watchstanders as they transfer around the fleet.

ELECTRONIC WARFARE AND CRYPTOLOGY

The sailors who run electronic warfare and cryptology systems aboard a ship are rated cryptologists (CTs). Due to the complexity and cost of the AN/SLQ-32 Electronic Warfare Suite, the operations officer should focus extra maintenance spot-checks on this system. The SLQ-32 system requires regular maintenance and quarterly testing using shore facilities. Another maintenance-intensive system is the Passive Countermeasures System (PCMS), whose maintenance cryptologic technicians will also manage. Because elements of PCMS can be found throughout the ship, the challenges of running a good PCMS maintenance program are similar to those of monitoring damage control. Strong PCMS petty officers are essential for a good program. This is an area where good management will lead to tactical advantage in combat, so prioritize accordingly. The electronic warfare division also handles ordnance—including chaff and Nulka (two types of antiship missile decoys).

Another aspect of the cryptologist rate is manning and operating the ship's Signals Exploitation Space (SSES) on those ships equipped with it. A limited-duty officer or chief warrant officer typically manages this program. Due to the isolated location of SSES equipment and operations, it can be easy for the assigned CTs to remain behind the "green door." Ops should therefore make it a priority to keep the cryptographers "on the team," and include them in everything from CIC training to duty sections and working parties.

The classification of SSES operations ensures that the CT's work gets limited visibility. Ops should routinely tour the space and be involved with SSES tasking. A daily read-board of SSES-produced, top-secret intelligence traffic (for Ops and the CO, at a minimum) can help break the CTs out of SSES and expose good petty officers to the chain of command.

INTELLIGENCE

Nearly all of the ship's activities—from lookout identification of a passing ship to post-visit cataloging of a foreign port's amenities—generate intelligence. Ops can play a key role in creating a mind-set for a ship's intelligence, which is neither a by-product nor an afterthought. In order to fulfill the vision of each naval unit as a node in a network and take full advantage of the Navy's presence mission, intelligence gathering needs to be second nature. Key contributors to the war on terrorism, Navy ships offer the most persistent platforms for intelligence, surveillance, and reconnaissance.

To small ships the Navy typically assigns an enlisted intelligence assistant from the intelligence specialist (IS) rating. This sailor should be familiar with off-ship requirements, and plays a key role in the strike group's intelligence network. Other ships will develop a collateral duty intelligence officer (CDIO), typically as an additional duty for the CIC officer. All intelligence personnel should be intimately familiar with the intelligence warfare area requirements in the SFTM. As a team goal for the department, operations officers should strive to earn the Navy's Intelligence Excellence Award. Base your goal on the citation from the previous winner in the appropriate ship class, and model your intelligence gathering and reporting efforts accordingly. Practicing intelligence reporting and looking for opportunities to contribute to intelligence collection may pay dividends for the ship's reputation. Ops should review key intelligence-related areas such as lookout training and qualification, Global Command and Control System-Maritime (GCCS-M) reporting, ship-locator reports, intelligence and information reports, and port-visit, after-action reports. Even minimal oversight by the operations officer in these areas can result in improved performance.

COMMUNICATIONS DIVISION

Recent changes in maintenance and material management (3-M) mandated the organizational transfer of the communications division from the operations department to the combat systems department. Nevertheless, Ops should remain in close sync with communications—especially regarding the receipt and transmission of message traffic. After all, in today's information-driven, technology-based world, connectivity is the lifeblood of ship operations. Operations officers need to establish clear guidelines and priorities for circuit maintenance, restoration, and notification. In the event of a communications breakdown, Ops must understand the ship's capabilities and restoral procedures in order to redirect urgent communications and provide estimated times of repair to the CO and other ships. If, for example, a voice circuit is down for fifteen minutes, the communications watch team should notify Ops and the tactical action officer in CIC, if they are not already involved. A simple three- or four-circuit list, including maximum outage times, can be posted in radio central for the communications watch team to utilize. "Ops Circuit Priorities" can either be listed separately from the communications plan or included in the cover letter. In either case, Ops' priorities should always include data-links, and, in this regard, work closely with the combat systems officer.

Maintenance and Material Management (3-M) and the Current Ship's Maintenance Project (CSMP)

In an era of limited budgets and fewer ships, it is imperative to maintain the Current Ship's Maintenance Project (CSMP), an online database that directly feeds the equipment pillar of DRRS-N through the shore file. Division officers and chief petty officers must be active in the writing and review of CSMP jobs. Zone inspections and maintenance should feed the operations department's CSMP; the department head, meanwhile, should pay particular attention to the deck division and the PCMS work center.

Tracking and executing situational maintenance checks (R-checks) can be challenging. Most of the ship's major equipment requires pre-departure maintenance checks, including tuning radars and checking the anchor. Preparing pre-underway check-off lists and printing out all of the R-checks for a particular work center can help track these requirements. To ensure that such work is done, Ops should enlist the assistance of chief petty officers.

Operations Department Manning

Due to budget cuts, force reductions, optimal manning experiments, and less-dedicated training during the last decade, manning the fleet is increasingly a challenge. By defining key terms and covering the manning process, this section provides department heads with tools with which to address personnel shortfalls.

The manning control authority (U.S. Fleet Forces Command) sets the Navy's desired level of personnel readiness for surge capability and deployment. Navy Personnel Command (Pers-4013) (which recently replaced the Enlisted Placement Management Center or EPMAC) provides ships with sailors based on feedback from each ship's crew, its immediate superior (ISIC), and the type commander (which comprise the administrative chain of command). To communicate current and projected manning the Personnel Bureau first sends to each ship an Enlisted Distribution Verification Report (EDVR). The personnel officer checks the accuracy of the EDVR and provides feedback on a monthly basis. As the ship approaches the sustainment phase and deployment, a Personnel Manning Report (PERSMAR) is sent to the Bureau of Personnel. This report is a detailed assessment of current and projected manning intended to highlight the ship's most important manning needs for deployment overseas.

Each ship has several manning levels. For example, the Ship's Manning Document (SMD) delineates wartime manning requirements. The Manning Control Authority "pays" for manning by allotting billets, a number referred to as billets authorized (BA), or a ship's "places." Based on EDVRs, the Navy Manning Plan (NMP) dictates a crew's allotted number of "faces," or its "fair share" of available manning. In reality, due to training requirements, unplanned losses, expiring enlistments, and transfers, a ship typically carries fewer sailors, a number referred to as Current Onboard (COB). The manning system works best when projected nine months ahead—an estimate referred to in the EDVR as "projected onboard in nine months," or POB9. Adjusting to conflicting COB and NMP figures and the long wait to achieve POB9 manning is a constant source of frustration for ship commanders, and needs to be addressed early and often in the PERSMAR reports and through working-level engagement with enlisted detailers.

Ship commanders analyze manning on a number of levels, beginning with the basic crew size. They must also consider the ship's "fill," the number of sailors of a particular rate without consideration of pay grade, as well as its "fit," those with desired levels of expertise or leadership. For example, a ship's deck division may boast a dozen junior personnel, but no journeymen (E-5) or senior leaders (E-7 and above). Each ship, however, should have an appropriate mix of experts, journeymen, and apprentices in each assigned rate. Some sailors—such as air intercept controllers—have skills identified by a Navy Enlisted Classification (NEC) code. Responsible for determining each ship's "NEC Fit," or correct number of "mission essential or critical NECs," are the type commander and the Manning Control Authority.

For the department head, it is important to review the EDVR and identify shortages in fit, fill, and NECs. This information should be discussed with the executive officer and included in EDVR feedback and PERSMAR reporting. Manning issues should also be addressed during predeployment manning conferences. In the case of an unplanned loss, particularly of personnel with critical NECs such as search-and-rescue swimmers or air-intercept control supervisors, a ship's commander can request temporary additional duty assistance (TEMADD assist) through the ISIC. An Emergency Manning Inquiry Report (EMIR) should also be sent to the Personnel Bureau. Thinking ahead, proactive networking with the ISIC, TYCOM, and the Personnel Bureau can help alleviate, if not eliminate, a ship's shortage of correctly trained sailors.

Professional Tips:

- One important reference for the deck division is the Naval Ship's Technical Manual (NSTM), Volume II (chapter 631, "Surface Preparation," and chapter 634, "Decks").

- Use your network to obtain a copy of an unofficial but excellent Power Point brief prepared by the officers of USS *Donald Cook* entitled "Painting and Preservation."

- Seek opportunities to train.

- Once the ship is under way, coordinate with other vessels for CIC training.

- The relationship between Ops and the department-leading chief petty officer should mirror that of the CO and CMC.

- Use the Intelligence Excellence Award as a goal for your team.

- Despite not "owning" radio, Ops is responsible for ALL message traffic.

- Make circuit priorities and expectations known for each underway event, exercise, or operation as appropriate. Ensure that the communications watch team knows the mission priorities.

- Carefully check and spot-check situational maintenance (R-checks).

- Operations departments on cruiser- and destroyer-type ships (CRUDES, or "crew-dez") have less equipment and therefore fewer maintenance issues than engineering and combat systems departments. Ops may therefore need to strongly advocate for maintenance money. A good relationship with the port engineer and SMMO helps.

- PERSMAR reporting is governed by Commander, Fleet Forces Command and Commander, Navy Personnel Command Instruction 1300.1, Enlisted Manning Policy and Procedures, dated September 9, 2005.

- Consult with enlisted detailers and rating assignment officers of your professional network in order to fully grasp the Navy's manning availability and goals and to better advocate for your ship.

CHAPTER 5

ROUTINE
OPERATIONS

BLUF:

- *Smooth operations at sea depend on the personal attention of the operations officer.*
- *Know every detail of the ship's schedule of events.*
- *Manage the transitions. Personally supervise preparation and execution between events.*

A LANDING CRAFT, AIR-CUSHIONED LAUNCHES FROM AN LHD
WHILE IN PORT DARWIN, AUSTRALIA 2005. PHOTOGRAPHED FROM
THE FANTAIL OF USS CHANCELLORSVILLE.

Author's collection. (Mike Hellard)

Developing a Schedule of Events (SOE)

As discussed in chapter 3, your underway schedule of events should habitually include training sessions. Some ships, for example, regularly conduct navigation exercises, set general quarters and material condition Zebra, and conduct man-overboard drills each time they go to sea. Ops should dedicate extra time to each event that is supported by services, ATG, or interaction with other units. And it is good practice to plan a backup event in case the services fall through or a material casualty prevents the one planned. Finally, if the calendar permits, set aside time to practice future events.

The next step in developing the SOE is to check time and distance requirements. The Plan of Intended Movement (PIM) should be plotted on the appropriate charts, with priority given to events involving other units. The ship's reputation will be based in large part on punctuality and preparedness for refueling, formation steaming, tactical exercises, and other events. Propulsion-limiting engineering exercises offer superb training but must not prevent the ship from reaching a rendezvous point. Operating areas for gunshoots or tail operations, meanwhile, are active (or "hot") only for limited periods; the time and distance required to utilize these windows must therefore be carefully plotted on the chart. Allow the ship extra time for widely dispersed events, and arrive early when possible. A successful SOE is 95 percent preparation and 5 percent execution.

Preparing for Departure

Communications plans should reflect circuits and priorities for upcoming operations, and if possible, all voice and data circuits should be checked prior to departure. With the communications division now part of the combat systems department rather than directly under operations, extra care must be taken to ensure that a well-coordinated plan is presented to the captain. Additionally, Ops should get "a chop," a chance to review and offer input on the communications plan.

About an hour before sailing, Ops will make the following announcement: "Department Heads make readiness for sea reports to the Executive Officer in the pilothouse." This means that the department's spaces are secure; all personnel are accounted for; required pre-underway maintenance is complete; and the department is ready to head out to sea. Each division in the Ops department should maintain thorough checklists. Individual knowledge of how to prepare for sea duty is only useful until something is forgotten or until that crew member transfers. Ensure that your division officers report their readiness to you, walk your spaces, and report confidently to the XO that your department is ready for sea.

It is always important to walk your spaces daily, but doubly so prior to getting under way. While doing so, first check for cleanliness and stowage for sea. If evidence suggests that no one has swept the deck, get the chiefs involved immediately. Ensure that the appropriate material condition is set, and as you climb ladders inspect the ladder-backs, safety pins, safety chains, and cleanliness of the scuttles and other fittings. Pause at the top of each ladder to inspect cableways and overheads for accumulated dust. Schedule a blow-down or other deep-cleaning action when appropriate. When walking topside, examine lifelines and ensure that damage control and cleaning gear is stowed properly. Many eyes will be on the ship as it departs the naval station, and its reputation depends on a smart appearance.

ROUTINE UNDERWAY

Ships typically start the training phase by conducting independent operations, or Independent Steaming Exercises (ISE). Each ship's crew will establish habits quickly. If yours fails to establish a "battle rhythm," consult with the captain and ask his preference for instituting one. As defined by Naval

Warfare Publication (NWP) 5-01, *Navy Planning*, chapter 1.7, battle rhythm is "a process where the commander and staff synchronize the daily operating tempo within the planning, decision, execution, and assessment cycle to allow the commander to make timely decisions. This battle rhythm is the commander's battle rhythm. It is his 'plan of the day.' Furthermore, battle rhythm is a cascading process. The higher headquarters establishes a battle rhythm and, within this, the naval commander and subordinate commanders nest their own battle rhythm."

The capstone event of the ship's battle rhythm is the daily brief, also known as the "OPS/INTEL Brief." This meeting covers the upcoming 24–48 hours of operations and any real or exercise intelligence that affects them. Generally scheduled according to the CO's preference, daily briefs are typically held directly before or after the evening meal. A second element of the ship's battle rhythm is the production of daily reports by the operational chain of command, the primary one being Operational Report 5, or OPREP-5. The OPREP-5 is often called "OPREP-5 feeder" because it "feeds" the operational commander supervising the ship the required information for production of the OPREP-1 Operational Summary Report (OPSUM).

No schedule will remain intact. Changing weather, equipment issues, range-foulers (a ship that crosses into a live gunnery exercise), and other complications require that operations officers anticipate interruptions and monitor their impact with the chain of command. The OPS/INTEL brief is a good opportunity to brief most watchstanders, although it will likely require Ops' personal involvement.

Each evening a commanding officer's night orders wrap up the day's battle rhythm and lay out the plan for the period extending from the last event of one day to the first event of the next—usually from after the evening meal to the following day's breakfast. In preparing the night orders, Ops should utilize his peer networks to ascertain, and share with the crew, the context of the ship's operating area (locations of known fleet units and their intentions, etc.) and resolve potential problems such as two vessels competing for space in the same "night steam box." The night orders also offer an opportunity for Ops to insert training guidance or lessons learned the previous day.

Even when everything is proceeding smoothly, it is the operations officer's duty to manage transitions and make sure that the ship is set up for success. Ops should be present for watch turnovers during key events. In a three-section watch rotation, Ops should visit the bridge at the end of each watch to ensure that key events are being tracked. He or she should check the latest time and distance calculations and ensure that the CIC is providing forceful backup to the bridge navigation team's calculations. For critical rendezvous such as refueling, the watch immediately preceding an event is especially critical to successful execution. Ops' presence will keep the bridge team on their toes and focused.

Coordinated Exercises and Strike Group Training

The simplest coordinated event (such as deck-landing qualifications [DLQs] with the ship's assigned helicopter detachment) involves just two units, but should nevertheless be properly coordinated—beginning with a pre-exercise coordination message ("pre-ex") dispatched to all participating and supporting units to clearly establish the time, place, required communications, etc.

More complex training events, such as missile-firing or sinking exercises, may require letters of instruction (LOI), which should be read in detail and discussed ahead of time. Known as "group sails," multi-ship exercises conducted in the basic phase of training may utilize a published schedule of events (SOE), and designate specific units for providing pre-ex messages. One particularly useful type of group sail includes "revolver" events. In these, services are coordinated to support multiple ships in turn; as each ship completes an event, they rotate like a revolver chamber to the next. Revolver events are an efficient means of scheduling services or rotating training teams.

In the intermediate and advanced phases of training, ships will conduct Comprehensive Task Unit Exercises (COMPTUEX) and Joint Task Force Exercises (JTFEX). The former was once a scripted exercise with a known SOE; but now both are "free-play" exercises designed to test the individual units as well as the strike group staff. Rather than relying on pre-ex messages during these exercises, ships transition to governing operational tasking orders (OPTASKS) to respond as they will when deployed. Both COMPTUEX and JTFEX will challenge the operations officer's stamina. Ops' ability to keep up with the battle rhythm while standing a tactical watch and keeping the ship on task will be challenged during this multi-week event. To prevent debilitating fatigue, off-watch time must be managed judiciously—but not at the expense of administrative tasks necessary to watch duty. Put the ship's mission first and delegate to the maximum extent possible.

Returning to Port

After any underway the operations officer should review both met and unmet objectives. Lessons learned should be compiled and, if appropriate, officially submitted to the Navy Lessons Learned database. Additionally, after-action reports and "Bravo Zulu" messages (traditional messages meaning "well done") should be sent. In a strike group environment Ops will also be asked to attend a "hot wash" session in which leading participants review and discuss the operation or exercise's underway period.

Immediately upon returning to port, Ops must re-engage with the shore network to ensure that the ship is berthed correctly and ready to support the naval station as required. For example, if the ship's captain is the CO on the pier, the ship's crew will assume Pier SOPA (Senior Officer Present, Afloat) duties as prescribed in the local SOPA Manual.

PROFESSIONAL TIPS:

- Compare the operations department's pre-underway preparations and check-off list with the engineer's Master Light-Off Checklist (MLOC) for thoroughness and accountability. Ensure that the completed checklist is returned for review.

- Schedule training based on PBFT input.

- If using the TORIS/TFOM system, review it carefully for training requirements coming due.

- Resist the temptation to overload the schedule.

- Rendezvous with the oiler—not at a latitude and longitude point.

- Maintain continuous communication with other ships and service providers.

- It is good practice to verify an upcoming event with the service provider one day prior.

- Always work two watches and three events ahead on the schedule.

- A key distinction in an SOE is maneuvering versus non-maneuvering drills and exercises.

- Your ship's reputation is based on timeliness, readiness, and smart communications.

- Brief upcoming events at the Ops/Intel brief. Debrief those same events at the next Ops/Intel brief in order to capture and share lessons learned.

- Ensure 100 percent attendance at Ops/Intel for all watchstanders not actually on watch.

- When working with a squadron, consider a group sail with revolver events to maximize service availability and training team usage.

CHAPTER 6

MANAGEMENT PART II:
MESSAGES AND BRIEFS

BLUF:

- *Ops should be the subject matter expert on naval messages.*

THE DEPARTMENT HEADS AND OPERATIONS LIMITED DUTY OFFICER IN USS BENFOLD, 2003. ALL THREE LINE OFFICERS ARE IN COMMAND OR EXECUTIVE OFFICERS FLEETING-UP TO COMMAND AS OF THIS WRITING.
Author's collection. (Ed Gawaran)

MESSAGE TRAFFIC

ESSAGE TRAFFIC IS THE PRIMARY MEANS of communications between naval units. Composing accurate messages is therefore extremely important for scheduling, coordinating, and obtaining permission to carry out the ship's operations. The operational and administrative chains of command determine your home port's reporting requirements. The primary document for guidance from the operational commander is the Operations Order (OPORDER). Each fleet commander promulgates an OPORDER that details reporting requirements based on that commander's responsibilities. Administratively, regional and naval station commanders provide guidance through Senior Officer Present Afloat (SOPA) Administration Manuals (sometimes called SOPA Admin). In order to schedule and receive approval for everything from a departure time to conducting gunnery exercises or mooring to a buoy, Ops must be familiar with both lines of guidance.

Responsibility for preparing a message generally lies with the division officer responsible for each event. In the case of mooring to a buoy, for example, this might mean that the ship's first lieutenant will route a draft (either personally or electronically) through the "chop chain" of department heads, the executive officer, and then the captain for "release," or approval. As a courtesy to a new commanding officer, the drafter should deliver hard copies of even routine messages with the relevant references in order to establish the validity of the ship's procedures. Following approval by the CO, the message is delivered to the communications center ("radio") for transmission. Ops should ensure that this center dispatches messages according to a standard operating procedure (SOP). Distinct SOPs may be desired for different types of messages, such as responses to American Red Cross notifications or unit situation reports.

REVIEWING MESSAGE TRAFFIC

After scanning a particular message's references, check its content for the following:

1. Classification markings.
2. Precedence (this message is routine).

3. The date-time group (DTG). Time is in Zulu, not local.

4. Plain language addresses (PLADs); note that shore commands end with double-slashes and have office codes, sea commands do not.

5. Rank order of action and information addressees (in the INFO line, this sample goes from four-star command to three-star to two-star then one-star and O-6 command). Note the difference between COMDESRON (the commander and his staff) and DESRON (the collective, or all the ships in the squadron).

6. Proper message identification in the MSGID line (an administrative message).

7. Proper serialization—001, 001A, 001B, etc. for follow-ups.

8. The remarks section, which must end with a double slash (//).

9. If a classified message, a declassification date must follow the remarks section.

10. Declassification instructions must include a date for such action; a good rule of thumb is one year from the message's origination date.

For practice, review these items in the following, unclassified sample message:

(1) Message classification will be in the header and routing instructions found above the date-time group, but not shown here.
(2) R (3) 241242Z JUN 11
FM (4) COMNAVSURFLANT NORFOLK VA//N00//
TO USS SHIP
INFO (5) COMUSFLTFORCOM NORFOLK VA//N00//
COMSECONDFLT
COMNAVSURFLANT NORFOLK VA//N00//
COMCARSTRIKGRU TEN
COMDESRON TWO SIX
DESRON TWO SIX

BT
(1) UNCLAS
QQQQ
SUBJ: SAMPLE MESSAGE
(6) MSGID/GENADMIN,USMTF, 2007/
COMNAVSURFLANT/(7)001//
SUBJ/SAMPLE MESSAGE//
GENTEXT/REMARKS/(8)
1. BE DIRECT AND USE ACTIVE VOICE
2. KEEP IT SIMPLE
3. WHAT IS THE TASKING? WHEN IS THE DEADLINE?
4. IF THIS IS A RESPONSE MESSAGE, DOES IT ANSWER
THE QUESTION?//
(9), (10)
BT

"BT" indicates a "break in transmission." Many idiosyncrasies of message traffic originated in flag-hoist and voice communications.

For routine messages, it is a good idea to keep handy a file of templates, which provide the command duty officer with rough drafts of messages needed for reporting emergencies. When using a template, however, always note the date of its last update. Under normal circumstances, Ops should read and review all messages. It is a good idea to read the references and review the templates before approving them for use.

Administrative Reports

Messages administratively cover all aspects of the ship's operations, and are required for every aspect of a ship's movement from port to sea and back again. Logistics Requirements (LOGREQs, "log-recks") are submitted by Ops to provide the port operations officer with the schedule and services necessary for departure and arrival. Movement reports (MOVREPS, or "move-reps") detail the ship's planned movements and provide a general location of ship operations. They are also used to request weather support and optimal track ship's routing (O-T-S-R) for port-to-port transit. While the ship is under way, operations report five (OPREP-5, or "op-rep five") provides data on communications, personnel, fuel, and food. When the ship is steaming in company with other ships, these data are compiled in an operational summary report (OPSUM or OPREP-1) for the operational chain of command.

Planned exercises often require notification or permission from SOPA or the command in charge of range safety. For example, permission is required for use of a training anchorage or for firing large-caliber weapons. Exercises involving the support of another unit (or the use of communications, electronic warfare ranges, or aircraft) may require the filing of a service request. More elaborate events generally merit a pre-exercise (pre-ex) message detailing the officer conducting the exercise, a timeline, safety and coordinating information, and an explanation of the event itself. When in doubt, send a message written in plain language. Be prepared to brief the CO on your plan.

OPERATIONAL REPORTS (OPREPS)

Significant events are reported to the chain of command via Operational Report-3 (OPREP-3) or unit situation reports (Unit SITREPs). These messages detail specifics ranging from misconduct to personnel injuries to interaction with foreign military forces. The fleet commander and the OPNAVINST 3100.6 series provide the specific requirements and formats of such reports.

CASUALTY REPORTING (CASREPS)

Equipment degradation and casualties are tracked via casualty reports (CASREPs, or "caz-reps"). Categorized according to degree of severity, CASREPs should offer a clear picture of what system is broken, what efforts were made to fix it, and the parts and assistance still needed to complete repairs. Ops should review all CASREPs for consistency in schedules and impact, as well as specific reporting guidance from the strike group commander or ISIC.

DEFENSE READINESS REPORTING SYSTEM-NAVY (DRRS-N)

Having replaced the Status of Readiness and Training System (SORTS) message, the DRRS-N (or "dirs-en") feeds a joint, armed forces database. DRRS-N is Web-based and designed to track readiness online in five areas: personnel, equipment, training, supply, and ordnance. Various reporting systems, including CASREPs, feed the DRRS-N program to produce a metric-based computation of readiness. Commands are then required to provide a self-assessment of readiness with an explanation of any differences between calculated readiness and the unit assessment.

BRIEFS, POWER POINTS, AND MEMOS

As a first-tour department head you may have occasion to provide a face-to-face brief to a senior officer or staff; on your second tour you can expect to brief frequently. Time is a key factor, both for you in preparing the brief and for the senior officer in receiving and reviewing it. First, determine the target audience and their level of familiarity with the topic. All briefs should answer the W5H questions: Who? What? Why? When? Where? and How? For each, start with the Bottom Line Up Front (BLUF). When preparing projector slides, ask yourself if each answers a specific question and stays on message.

A good briefing requires more than mastery of Power Point, the standard tool for preparing and presenting slides. Ensure that your images convey your message; keep them clear and concise by using bullet points rather than full sentences. For example, one slide might address the background of the issue at hand; another may lay out your assumptions. Others could cover the metrics of the issue and how costs or trade-offs can be measured or compared. Wrap up your brief by reiterating the desired goal and how to achieve it. Be clear about what you want the audience to do with the information you provide.

Each staff likely uses a briefing format tailored to the commander. However, some standards apply. Briefs will generally include the issue (BLUF), background, discussion, and action or way ahead. You must master not only the format your boss prefers but also that of the ISIC. Briefs should also be just what their name implies—brief. Spend no more than one to two minutes on each slide, and use no more than ten slides. When possible, use graphs, charts, and tables to convey your message, and tailor your information to the audience. Communicating with efficiency is a skill that can be learned. Keeping your memos and e-mails succinct and professional will distinguish them from the seemingly innumerable unstructured, informal and wordy notes.

PROFESSIONAL TIPS:

- Personally deliver all messages with the required references to a newly reported CO for at least two weeks; thenceforth, deliver all non-routine messages until otherwise directed.

- NWP 1-03.1, Operational Reports, is the resource for casualty reports, search-and-rescue reports, mishap reports, Change of Operational Control (CHOP) reports, movement reports, and others. Start here when building message templates.

- Teach your division officers to write with the reader in mind.

- Ensure that the ship's message is consistent.

- Review messages not generated by the operations department for classification, schedule, and language.

- Review unclassified messages with an eye toward preventing electronic spillage—the passing of classified information over unclassified computer networks.

- Review messages after release by the CO in order to learn his or her writing style.

- Routing messages to the CO via junior officers does not absolve the originating department of responsibility for their contents and timeliness.

- You may want to contribute to every message sent from the ship, but do not hold up its routing to do so.

CHAPTER 7

DEPLOYMENT AND WARFIGHTING

BLUF:

- *Pre-deployment preparation is crucial to your effectiveness as a watchstander and planner.*
- *Prepare the other tactical action officers and the CIC watch team for the expected battle rhythm.*

RUSSIAN TU-142 BEAR ESCORTED BY CVW-5 AIRCRAFT, FLYING OVER USS CHANCELLORS-VILLE IN THE SEA OF JAPAN, 2005.

U.S. Navy photo.

PREPARING FOR DEPLOYMENT

THE PRE-DEPLOYMENT WORK-UP CYCLE will include various in-port training events and conferences. For example, computer simulations called Fleet Synthetic Training offer excellent preparation for communications work and watchstanding. Warfare Commander's Conferences provide opportunities to meet other operations officers as well as key personnel in the strike group network. During these, and other, similar sessions the strike group commander lectures on deployment and tactical expectations, and addresses issues related to pre-planned responses.

A reduced readiness condition granted by the TYCOM, a pre-overseas movement (POM) is a stand-down period during which up to 50 percent of crews on continental United States (CONUS)– and Hawaii-based ships are allowed to depart on leave. Under these conditions, operations officers must be careful not to allow the ninety-day, TORIS/TFOM rolling window of readiness to degrade unexpectedly (see chapter 3). Be sure that TORIS/TFOM projections are understood and acknowledged by the other department heads and accounted for in leave plans; do your best to allow crew members maximum time for leave. To limit the risk of having to sail without all qualified personnel, maintain an emergency sortie watchbill, which should identify gaps in critical personnel and annotate coverage when available. For example, each ship has only one independent duty corpsman who must arrange for another qualified corpsman as a stand-in while on leave.

Those crew members that remain on board during a POM should keep busy working from a POM checklist (provided by the type commander), performing maintenance and repairs, stocking up on consumable items, and generally preparing for the six-to-eight-month (or longer) deployment ahead. Returning deployers with similar assignments should share any lessons learned. To make sure that they miss nothing, Ops can consult his or her network of operations officer peers or seek guidance from strike group or squadron commanders.

The Ops Boss

Ships deployed overseas spend the vast majority of their time conducting operations. As the operations officer, the better prepared you are, the greater effect you will have as a watchstander and as an advocate for your ship within the strike group or, if your ship deploys independently, at the theater level. A working understanding of geopolitical concerns, theater intelligence and engagement requirements, and the operational law goals of the numbered fleet commander will help make your ship a valuable contributor to the Navy mission in the region.

In most cases, a ship will actually cross from one fleet commander's area of responsibility to another's, and possibly even a third, during a single deployment. The operations officer must be thoroughly familiar with all of the guidance in each theater in order to seamlessly transition through this change of operational control (CHOP). During the ship's transit, Ops should rehearse the battle rhythm of the destination theater. Each fleet commander maintains a Web site with the most recent information about that theater; review it, and ensure that all watchstanders are familiar with the fleet's procedures, requirements, and expectations.

TASK ORGANIZATION

A fleet is typically organized into task forces, the organization of which its commander promulgates in a General Operational Information (OPGEN) message. (Dispersed quarterly, or when major units CHOP in and out, this is essentially a roster of players.)

Task force designations are fairly standard. For example, CTF 70 and CTF 50 are carrier task forces in their respective fleets, while CTF 23, 33, 43, 53, 63, and 73 are logistical forces in their respective numbered fleets. Subordinate to the task force is the task group. For example, if Seventh Fleet contains two carrier strike groups, one will be Task Group 70.1 and the other Task Group 70.2. To each task group is assigned a number of task units (TU) and their subordinate task elements (TE). Designation as a task force, group, unit, or element depends on the mission assigned by the fleet rather than the size of the unit. A ship may be designated a task unit or task element, or both, at the same time. For example, a cruiser assigned air defense commander duties might be TU 70.1.2 with the duties of Redcrown, Force Track Data Coordinator, and the helicopter detachment (all residing on board) assigned as subordinate task elements. These designations can be sources of motivation for watchstanders who may not otherwise realize their importance to the strike group.

OPERATIONS ORDER (OPORDER)

Each fleet describes its organization and operating principles in published guidance. Start familiarizing yourself with the fleet in your area by reading its OPORDER cover to cover—including the annexes and appendixes, which contain important information.

OPTASKs are instructions for conduct in antisubmarine, surface, anti-air, and other warfare areas. Review the Navy-wide OPTASK first and see how your strike group or theater's standing OPTASK differs from it. Through supplemental guidance (OPTASK SUPP), OPTASKs can be modified for specific time periods or mission areas.

Intentions messages provide warfare commanders with tactical assessments and present plans for the immediate future. Strike group commanders typically provide daily intentions messages (DIMS); others release them on a weekly basis as WIMS. Special intentions (SPINS) are dispatched as needed.

An extremely efficient process for disseminating important elements of daily message traffic to the wardroom and chiefs' mess is the "DIMS Digest." By simply cutting and pasting useful portions of all the daily messages into a single, pointed e-mail, Ops can provide the ship's key watchstanders with a single source of maintenance, logistics, operations, and planning information that multiple departments normally cull from a variety of sources. Credit for this idea belongs to USS *Higgins.*

Operational Law (OPLAW)

Generally covered in the OPORDERS, legal issues sometimes require interpretation. Most U.S. Navy ships do not sail with Judge Advocate General (JAG) officers on board. However, a JAG corps officer attached to the strike group or the TYCOM staff is intimately involved in developing operational guidance and advising commanders of the legal implications of fleet operations. And the staff judge advocate, known as the "S-J-A" or simply as "Judge," should brief your crew prior to deployment. It is incumbent on the operations officer to understand the basics of operational law and to ensure that any of the CO's concerns are addressed. Remember, SJA advice is only a phone call away. Potential legal issues include:

Rules of Engagement (ROE), which are codified in the Chairman, Joint Chiefs of Staff Instruction, are generally divided into two types: rules for self-defense and supplemental rules for mission accomplishment. This document defines the key terms associated with self-defense ROE and explicitly states that a unit commander has the inherent right and obligation of self-defense when faced with a hostile act or demonstration of hostile intent. Absent the former, the ship's commander must attempt to determine the latter. If warning shots or other steps do not produce clear results, explicit guidance should be sought. In general, ROE are permissive in nature, and authorize deadly force in cases of self-defense. All tactical watchstanders should pay special attention to the distinctions between individual, unit, and collective self-defense. Mission specific ROE are classified.

In contrast to ROE, the Rules for the Use of Force (RUF) are restrictive in nature and generally apply only within the territorial waters of the United States (including ships in U.S. ports). They authorize the use of deadly force only as a last resort (or when lesser means cannot be reasonably employed), and direct military personnel to respond to threats with a gradual escalation from verbal commands to the use of firearms—a similar policy to that followed by police officers.

It is imperative that armed watchstanders understand the difference between force protection overseas and back home.

Law of the Sea

While the United States has not signed the United Nations Convention on the Law of the Sea (UNCLOS), the Navy adheres to the treaty's provisions. UNCLOS defines internal waters, baselines, territorial seas, contiguous zones, and exclusive economic zones, as well as rules under which ships and aircraft must operate in these areas.

Freedom of Navigation

In customary law, rights must be asserted and our strict adherence to transit and innocent passage regimes builds our legal case. Ships may be called upon to assert the rights of the United States under international law through Freedom of Navigation operations (FONOPS). Pay strict attention to Fleet Operations Orders for FONOPS requirements and reporting.

JOINT OPERATIONS

By definition, any activity, organization, or operation is a joint one when it includes two or more U.S. military services. These services are integrated in a task force organization in order to provide the greatest capability in certain functions that are common to all operations. Joint forces support each other with command and control, intelligence, fires, movement and maneuver, protection, and sustainment. Joint operations can be anything from missile defense, to air-to-air refueling, to embarking Army helicopters. In any such operation, planning, communications, and data links are the keys to effectiveness.

Due to the number of countries in the region with large and proficient navies, joint operations that focus on Navy missions typically take place in the western Pacific theater. Here, Seventh Fleet conducts joint operations that support the combatant commander's strategic goals. For example, Navy ships embark Army helicopters in Counter-Special Operations Forces Exercises (CSOF-EX). And only in Seventh Fleet do Air Force strike fighters practice maritime interdiction. In others, joint operations focus almost exclusively on land-based, special operations required by the combatant commander.

Combined Operations

Actions involving coalition or allied military forces are called combined operations. Again, they require solid planning, communications, and data links, and typically employ liaison officers (or "L-N-Os") to bridge language and procedural barriers.

Foreign disclosure issues should be considered well before embarking foreign military personnel. For guidance on this matter, fleet commanders depend on an especially knowledgeable staff officer whose sole job is to provide it. Ops should consult with the disclosure officer early and alert embarked personnel to information exchange boundaries. Mission success may depend on the ship's crew being a good host, but it should not come at the cost of comprising classified information.

Multinational cooperation in the antipiracy mission is the working model for combined operations. U.S. leadership is provided through Central Command and Fifth Fleet, but the head of Commander, Task Force 151, conducting operations in the waters around Somalia, rotates among the contributing navies. Navies from around the world, including Russia and China, have contributed to the operation, which offers a fine example of cooperation at sea.

Flagship Duties

Whether embarking U.S. or foreign staffs, being a good host goes a long way toward mission success. In order to meet the expectations of the commodore or admiral, Ops should quickly liaison with the embarking staff and protocol officer. Work to make the staff as effective as possible, and consider how to balance its need for work space, communications, and individual watchstander requirements with the ship's organization. The staff embarkation plan should include disclosure requirements for classified information; some squadron staffs also rely on embarkation instructions. Regardless, it is a good idea to communicate directly with the last unit to host the staff and request any lessons learned.

On-Scene Commander

Every ship must be prepared to render assistance to a mariner in distress. Maintain a standard operating procedure, or at least a checklist, to which you can refer when aiding a disabled vessel or a man overboard. Regularly exercise the rescue-and-assistance detail bill to ensure that all hands understand their roles. Counter-piracy and counter-drug mission areas often include migrant or refugee routes, and encounters with unseaworthy vessels can be expected. Have a clear plan, therefore, for holding a large number of survivors or detainees.

Classified Contingency Operations

Ships are occasionally called upon to support classified, special warfare or cryptography-related missions, the details of which may keep the operations officer exceptionally busy. Ops should proactively implement "River City" (a program that limits e-mail and cell phone access) and other operations security (OPSEC) tools and reminders. Educate the crew (perhaps with the aid of the CO) as to what duty-related information is or is not allowed to be disclosed to families—particularly via social media—in order to prevent the unauthorized leak of information. A sample OPSEC page 13, administrative counseling for sailors, is provided in Appendix C.

War at Sea

While the days of ship-to-ship battle may have largely passed, we must continue to maintain our primary warfare capabilities. Training in wartime, particularly in today's single-mission environment, is necessary to maintain proficiency and readiness. To stimulate innovative thinking, rehearse tactics, and determine real vulnerabilities, the ship's training teams may regularly utilize simulated combat scenarios. For example, they might challenge a tactical watch team in a surprise drill to find out just how long air support would take to reach an area at a given time.

After Action

Just as it is a best practice to debrief evolutions such as sea and anchor or underway replenishment detail, it is also important to debrief deployment exercises, missions and combat. Lessons learned should be submitted for consideration both through the Navy Lessons Learned database and as feedback to the operational commander.

Professional Tips:

- Beware of the 90-day, rolling window for TORIS/TFOM during Pre-Overseas Movement (POM) stand-downs, holidays, and post-deployment leave and upkeep.

- Neither you nor your sailors will have time to read all references while deployed, so prior preparation is essential.

- Keep important information organized and within arm's reach of all watchstanders, either by utilizing old-school, three-ring binders or an electronic version on a shared drive.

- Utilize a DIMS Digest to ensure that key personnel are informed as to on-fleet and task force requirements, intentions, and schedules.

- A quiet CIC is most conducive to effective operations.

- Planning conferences are essential to any complex operation—and doubly so for combined operations. At a minimum, Ops should consider the following: Initial Planning Conferences (IPC), Mid-term Planning Conferences (MPC), Final Planning Conferences (FPC), pre-sail conferences, and hot wash/post-exercise conferences.

- The best reference for OPLAW concerns is the *Commander's Handbook on the Law of Naval Operations*, NWP 1-14M.

CHAPTER 8

MANAGEMENT PART III:
COLLATERAL DUTIES AND AWARDS

BLUF:

- *Collateral duties must not become primary ones.*
- *Early planning and delegation are keys to successful management.*

USS DEVASTATOR LANDS IN SAN DIEGO, CALIFORNIA, COMPLETING A HOMEPORT SHIFT FROM INGLESIDE, TEXAS, 2009.

U.S. Navy photo.

A N OPERATIONS OFFICER'S COLLATERAL DUTIES may include those of safety officer, security manager, annual awards coordinator, and senior watch officer—the latter of which is a leadership role that will test any department head's organizational skills. Governed by Navy instructions and type commander guidance, the safety, security, and awards programs are evaluated at the end of the calendar year based on specific requirements, which are discussed in the following sections.

An effective strategy for planning and executing the aforementioned programs, as well as for tracking eligibility for annual awards, is "reverse planning." To be effective, these programs must complete x, y, and z during the year. The requirement needed to complete those tasks is known in advance and prior preparation will lead to success. For maximum efficiency, incorporate reverse planning into the format of the plan of actions and milestones (POAMs) discussed in chapter 2.

SAFETY OFFICER

Responsible for risk management and establishing safety procedures that help assure mission success, the safety officer performs an important collateral duty that contributes to sailors' quality of service. He or she must not become bogged down in excess administrative work (known as "administrivia").

The best way to make safety part of the ship's culture is to lay out the safety program in detail before the start of the calendar year. Using the Green *E* criteria from the Surface Forces Training Manual, develop a POAM utilizing a tabbed binder. On scratch paper, list the requirements in calendar order—for instance, quarterly safety council meetings. Tab the binder by quarters and insert an attendance list with the required billets (CO, XO, CMC, etc., rather than names) and signature lines. Populate the binder using all the applicable instructions. Beginning this process while in the training pipeline or during holiday stand-downs can produce a generic plan that is 90 percent complete—one that you can adjust during the balance of the year. Delegating the program's day-to-day management to other safety personnel, such as the senior medical department representative and the assistant safety officer, frees the safety officer to track progress from the checklist and provide input to PBFT.

Remember that multiple instruction manuals discuss the Safety Program, and it is reviewed in detail during the Board of Inspection and Survey. The safety officer should therefore schedule a formal Navy Safety Center Survey and accommodate Safety Center visits when scheduled. Everything from gas-free engineering to motorcycle safety lies within the safety officer's responsibilities, so keeping abreast of the latest guidance is imperative.

In accordance with the Surface Forces Training Manual, operational risk management (ORM) is now evaluated during every observed training evolution. Ops should pay careful attention to briefs and debriefs in order to build awareness of risk management. Taking risks is sometimes worthwhile—even necessary—but they should never be accepted blindly. Risk decisions must be made at the proper level based on the recommendations of personnel most competent in the task at hand. The safety officer ensures that the commanding officer is made aware of the need for such decisions.

Conducting regular safety spot-checks is a good practice and several processes can be used. The maintenance and material management (3-M) system includes specific maintenance that only safety petty officers can perform. The safety officer should key on those tasks for spot-checks. Another safety aspect of the 3-M system is the quarterly requirement for the safety officer to review the Current Ship's Maintenance Plan (CSMP) for safety related jobs. The 3-M coordinator should print these out and review them at each PBFT.

Another good practice for the safety officer is to simply follow the in-depth, online checklists posted on the Board of Inspection and Survey's Web site. Under the material inspection/trial tab is a section labeled NAVOSH/EP: Navy

Occupational Safety and Health (NAVOSH) and environmental protection (EP) cover all of a ship's required safety programs.

SECURITY MANAGER

During the 1990s both the Secret Control Program and the Security Manager Program were reviewed during Command Inspection. Today's fleet lacks a formal, comprehensive program with which to review shipboard security, but Department of Defense guidelines require each unit to maintain a comprehensive information security program that includes physical security. (A sample instruction is provided as Appendix B.) The ship's security instructions should cover everything from securing doors and other entrances to safeguarding communications and classified material. In 2011, Cyber Command introduced the Cyber Security Inspection and Creditation Program that adds computer network security to physical and information security.

Each ship's information security program includes the Communications Security Management System, more commonly referred to as Electronic Key Material Systems (EKMS), which governs the use of communications security and cryptology-related equipment. The EKMS custodian, typically the communications officer, should be a meticulous manager with able assistants as alternate custodians. Recent revisions to EKMS guidelines require quarterly spot-checks by the XO and department head as well as the CO. At its core, EKMS is an accounting function; its checklists are comprehensive, and oversight of daily usage, monthly reports, and spot-checks is imperative. Fortunately, EKMS Advice and Assist Teams are generally available to answer relevant questions. While COMMO and EKMS typically work for the combat systems officer, the Ops department may be a local holder, and will certainly have EKMS users.

In addition to EKMS, ships must account for Top Secret and secret material and ensure proper safeguards. Each level of classification is assigned to an officer for accountability. The Top Secret control officer is usually the operations, cryptology, or strike officer. Controlling classified material outside the communications security world of EKMS still requires meticulous attention to detail. After all, the Top Secret classification implies that exposure of the relevant material could gravely threaten U.S. security. Similar to EKMS, Top Secret control is also essentially an accounting function. Fortunately, most ships carry minimal Top Secret material.

Inventories of such information, however, can get out of control, and ships should hold monthly reviews of their holdings to prevent this. The monthly report should include a list of new material received during the month, items destroyed during the last month, and items proposed for destruction. The report should also include the latest physical inventory as an enclosure. With the availability of classified material in electronic formats, physical holdings can and should be kept to a minimum.

Another often-overlooked aspect of security is Operations Security (OPSEC)—the essence of which is perhaps best expressed by the World War II slogan, "Loose lips sink ships." In a world filled with information technology, getting this message out to sailors and their families is increasingly important. A sample OPSEC—Administrative Counseling and Remarks for Sailors (known as a Page 13)—is provided as Appendix C.

SHIP AWARDS

The Battle Effectiveness competition is a yardstick for measuring ship performance. As with safety and security, planning for it should begin prior to the calendar year. Responsible departments should use award criteria to produce POAMs, which can be scheduled during a long-range planning meeting. Not every ship will win the "Battle E," but no crew should lose out by failing to plan all the events. In fact, if the ship's calendar proves exceptionally tight, early warning to and coordination with the ISIC might justify a waiver for a specific event.

SENIOR WATCH OFFICER

The Senior Watch Officer (SWO, or "swoh") is responsible for developing and proposing watch assignments for the commanding officer to approve. The CO must sign all underway and in-port watchbills that include armed watches. Another important duty of the SWO is to develop and execute a qualification plan for all junior officers, whom he or she is charged with shepherding toward qualification and preparing for events and boards. It is important to track which officers have had opportunities to practice quintessential ship-handling skills such as conning in and out of port or alongside a replenishment ship. Because junior officers and crew members particularly value watch assignments of every type, the SWO should assign officers to these events transparently. A second-tour division officer such as TRAINO can assist with this. Most SWOs also rely on a senior enlisted watchbill coordinator to provide the enlisted sailors for each watchbill. The senior enlisted watchbill coordinator position is a trusted one, and the SWO should monitor the proposed watch teams and ensure equitable assignments among the crew. The SWO is also required to have a watchbill (or watch team) replacement plan (WBRP/WTRP) for each watchbill. Maintaining the WBRP out four quarters beyond the current calendar quarter is a challenge, but worth the effort, as a good WBRP provides the foundation for future qualifications and watch rotations.

The most effective SWOs go beyond the paperwork. Since only the CO can approve changes to watchbills, the SWO should spot-check them for attendance and develop an understanding of the CO's comfort level with individual watchstanders. The SWO should, of course, recognize the strengths and weaknesses of all watchstanders in order to build effective teams. Generally assigned to the most senior department head, SWO duty offers a tremendous opportunity to mentor and coach junior officers and exhibit leadership skills. Those appointed to this position should make the most of the opportunity. Periodically sit down with the junior officers to discuss their qualification goals, and using a calendar and the ship's schedule, draft individual POAMs in order to track their progress and ensure timely qualifications.

Collateral duties require meticulous management—lack of attention to detail can transform a simple program into an unnecessarily time consuming duty. If a collateral task begins to take up all your time and energy as a department head, then your actual primary duty as operations officer is probably being neglected, and might put you in professional jeopardy.

PROFESSIONAL TIPS:

- Key collateral duties require extra effort and attention.

- In order to prevent collateral duties from becoming primary ones, delegate day-to-day functions to a competent, second-tour division officer and utilize a sharp chief petty officer as an assistant.

- The Naval Safety Center will conduct a safety survey and review the ship's safety program when requested. Ops should request a visit to the ship every thirty-six months.

- The Board of Inspection and Survey Web site address is: www.public.navy.mil/fltfor/insurv/pages/default.aspx (accessed on July 29, 2011).

- Competing for the Battle E is a never-ending process. As part of a POAM, Ops should continually remind crew members what will disqualify a ship as well as what will earn it distinction.

CHAPTER 9

LEADERSHIP AND THE BIG PICTURE

BLUF:

- *Approach your duties as you would command of your own ship.*
- *It takes twenty years to get twenty years of experience.*

RETIREMENT CEREMONY FOR MASTER CHIEF KEVIN WEINZIMMER ABOARD USS ALABAMA, 2007.

Author's collection.

D EPARTMENT HEAD TOURS are widely acknowledged as the most difficult in the surface warfare career path. They need not be so, as plenty of support is available. Recognize that gaining professional competence requires significant preparation and stamina. Once you have mastered being the Ops department's boss, you will be able to build a command perspective. The challenges and rewards of the operations officer role are good preparation for command at sea, as they encompass the leadership opportunities and require the management skills demanded inside and outside the ship's lifelines.

As you develop your command perspective you will begin to recognize in your processes or procedures where your ship may be vulnerable to risk. Even experienced crews can fall into traps. With proper leadership organizational pitfalls are preventable at every level in the chain of command.

Michael R. Adams' book, *Shipboard Bridge Resource Management* (Eastport, Maine: Nor'easter Press, 2006), details a number of causes—lack of situational awareness, stress, complacency, fatigue, miscommunication, a lack of teamwork, etc.—of mishaps, and postulates that an "error chain" can be traced backward from most major accidents. Breaking any link in that succession of errors may prevent a catastrophe. Organizations can track lessons learned with effective operational risk management, the briefing and debriefing of special evolutions, and other, more formal processes, and establish a culture of forceful backup to prevent error chains.

One potential contributor to the error chain (and another organizational trap) is a lack of procedural compliance. Complex organizations working under stressful conditions over long periods of time are susceptible to what author Scott A. Snook calls "practical drift"—the slow, steady, uncoupling of local practice from written procedure. In his book, *Friendly Fire: The Accidental Shootdown of U.S. Black Hawks over Northern Iraq* (Princeton: Princeton University Press, 2000), Snook analyzed the accidental shoot-down of two

Army helicopters over northern Iraq in 1991. He hypothesized about the conditions that increased the likelihood of such a mistake, and concluded that practical drift is a phenomenon common to many mishaps. You may hear practical drift verbalized as "That's the way we've always done it" in response to a request to produce a written reference. To avoid this trap, you must demand of your sailors verbatim compliance with procedures and thorough knowledge of technical manuals and tactical guidance, and frequently review references.

Admiral Harold W. Gehman Jr. identified another potential organizational pitfall in a December 7, 2005, speech at the U.S. Naval Academy. Entitled "Ethical Challenges for Organizations: Lessons Learned from the USS *Cole* and *Columbia* Tragedies" (http://www.usna.edu/Ethics/Publications/GehmanPg1-28_Final.pdf, accessed on July 7, 2011), Admiral Gehman's lecture laid out his investigation into the October 2000 bombing of the USS *Cole*. "They [the *Cole*'s force protection team] reduced the process down to its lowest common denominator," he noted. "I send off a message. I get an answer back. Therefore, we are protected from terrorists." They had put all the "checks in the boxes," he added, but their force protection training hadn't sunk in: "[O]ur investigation found that they essentially had gone through the motions. In other words, they had determined the minimum that needed to be done, and they had trivialized the whole event."

Trivialization can infiltrate any command; only constant reiteration of the mission, an ability to critique the organization from an outside perspective, and repeated review of the operational guidance can keep it at bay. It is better to openly discuss concerns over requirements than to allow sailors to decide for themselves whether or not that requirement is valid.

These three types of organizational traps—error chains, practical drift, and trivialization—are certainly not the only ones. But rigorous application of operational risk management will go a long way toward preventing accidents. Remember, a ship's mission is to fight. The mechanisms we use to train, track readiness, and enforce safety should always enhance—never diminish—our capabilities.

Finally, I offer a personal note. When I was a first-tour division officer, I inquired with the captain about the possibility of qualifying as a command duty officer. I offered enthusiasm and, as I saw it, demonstrated abilities and the willingness to seek assistance from a considerably more experienced Wardroom. "It takes twenty years to get twenty years' experience," he replied. At the time I felt stifled, but now, as I approach my twentieth year, I clearly see the wisdom in his statement. You probably do not have twenty years' experience as an operations officer, and therefore should not assume that you have seen it all or have all the answers. By the same token, don't be afraid to tap someone else's experience by asking questions, or to learn from your own mistakes.

PROFESSIONAL TIPS:

- Mishaps can befall anyone.

- The information with which to avoid mishaps is on board.

- Manage information so that the right people get the right information at the right time.

- Manage transitions and be present and alert during unsettled situations.

SUBJ: DESIGNATION AS FORCE TACTICAL ACTION OFFICER

1. Having completed Aegis Combat Systems Officer Track II and Force Air Defense Course at the Aegis Training and Readiness Center, Dahlgren, Virginia, and the Force Air Defense Commander Course with Aegis Training and Readiness Center Detachment Yokosuka, Japan, you have the pre-requisite training required for a Force Air Defense watchstation.

2. As the Air Defense Commander for KITTY HAWK Carrier Strike Group and Forward Deployed Naval Forces Expeditionary Strike Group, I have the trust and confidence in you to defend the force. I intend to coordinate all defensive measures designed to destroy, nullify, or reduce the effectiveness of attacking enemy aircraft or missiles. I expect you to aggressively establish and maintain air supremacy in the vital area and air superiority throughout the area of operations through the employment of defensive counter air aircraft and air defense units. Our aggressive defense will facilitate a rapid transition to offensive air operations. Similar to the ship's Tactical Action Officer, your authority is limited to defense of the force. You should make every effort to call me before employing defensive tactics, but do not wait for me to act if required for the safety of the force. I reserve the right to conduct offensive actions.

3. You are specifically charged with taking timely defensive measures to prevent coordinated or single threat aircraft, including reconnaissance flights, from entering the vital area unescorted or unengaged.

4. This is a significant qualification with Battle Force–wide responsibility.

5. Congratulations!

USS SHIP INSTRUCTION 5510.36

Subj: INFORMATION SECURITY PROGRAM

Ref: (a) SECNAVINST 5510.36 *DON Information Security Program Instruction*
      (b) SECNAV M-5510.36 *DON Information Security Program Manual*
      (c) OPNAVINST 3120.32C, *Standard Organization and Regulations of the U.S. Navy,* 11 Apr 94
      (d) EKMS-1, *CMS Policy and Procedures for Navy Electronic Key Management Systems (U),* 5 Oct 04
      (e) NTTP 1-01, *Naval Warfare Library,* Apr 05
      (f) USSAN 1-69, *United States Implementation of NATO Security Procedures,* 21 Apr 82
      (g) OPNAVINST 5239.1B, *Navy Information Assurance (IA) Program,* 9 Nov 99
      (h) OPNAVINST 5530.14C, *Navy Physical Security,* 10 Dec 98
      (i) SHIPINST 5530.1C, *Physical Security Plan,* [date]
      (j) SHIPINST 3301.1H, *USS SHIP Emergency Action Plan,* [date]

Encl: (1) Quarterly Notice of Information Security Program Assignments
       (2) Monthly report format (per ship requirements, not included in sample)

1. PURPOSE. Per reference (a), the Information Security Program (ISP) is designed to protect classified information through appropriate classification, proper safeguarding, secure transmission, and documented destruction. Reference (b) provides the guidelines for this command instruction.

2. RESPONSIBILITY. The Executive Officer is designated as the Command Security Manager and Command Security Officer. The Command Security Manager reports directly to the Commanding Officer on all matters relating to the protection of classified information per reference (c). The security manager is responsible for implementing this ISP. The security manager shall remain cognizant of all command information, personnel, and industrial security functions and ensure that the security program is coordinated and inclusive of all requirements of reference (b). The following personnel report to the Executive Officer in their duties to safeguard classified information:

a. **Top Secret Control Officer (TSCO).** The Operations Officer is designated TSCO. The TSCO shall:

(1) Maintain a system of accountability (e.g., registry) to record the receipt, reproduction, transfer, transmission, down-grading, declassification and destruction of command Top Secret information.

(2) Ensure that Top Secret material is inventoried monthly, or more frequently when circumstances warrant (see reference (b) chapter 7, paragraph 7-3) and reported to the Commanding Officer.

b. **Top Secret Control Assistant (TSCA).** The Communications Leading Chief Petty Officer is designated the TSCA. Typically the only Top Secret material on a minesweeper is that equipment associated with message traffic in radio central. A TSCA is designated to formally maintain the capacity for two-person integrity if required.

c. **Electronic Key Management System (EKMS) Manager.** The EKMS manager is the principal advisor to the commanding officer in all matters regarding the Communication Material System (CMS). Specific duties and responsibilities for the EKMS manager and any alternates are outlined in reference (d). Regular spot-checks shall be conducted in accordance with reference (d).

d. **Secret Control Officer (SCO).** The Operations Officer is designated SCO. The SCO shall:

(1) Maintain a system of accountability (e.g., registry) to record the receipt and destruction of command Secret information.

(2) Ensure that inventory spotchecks of Secret material are conducted monthly and reported to the Commanding Officer.

e. **Secret Control Clerk.** The Secret Control Clerk shall perform duties as required by the SCO.

f. **Naval Warfare Publications (NWP) Custodian**. Per reference (e), the NWP custodian will exercise control over receipt, correction, stowage, security, accounting, distribution, and authorized destruction of all NWPs.

g. **North Atlantic Treaty Organization (NATO) Control Officer**. The NATO control officer and alternate shall ensure that NATO information is correctly controlled and accounted for, and that NATO security procedures are observed. Reference (f) establishes procedures and minimum security standards for the handling and protection of NATO classified information. Transactions in the NATO Control account shall be reported monthly.

h. **Information Assurance Manager (IAM).** Per reference (g), the IAM serves as the point of contact for all command information assurance (IA) matters and implements the command's IA program. Working for the IAM, Information Assurance Officers (IAOs) are designated for each information system and network in the command, and are responsible for implementing and maintaining the command's information technology systems and network security requirements.

i. **Security Assistant**. The Ship's Secretary is designated as the Security Assistant and shall perform duties as required by the Security Manager.

3. RISK MANAGEMENT. USS SHIP will confront different operating environments and sets of changing operational requirements. Therefore, the security manager shall advise the

commanding officer on how best to apply risk management principles in order to attain the required levels of protection. Employing risk management may result in command decisions to adopt specific security measures given the relative costs and available resources. Additionally, the security manager shall:

a. Report and investigate loss, compromise, and other security discrepancies in accordance with Chapter 12 of reference (a).

b. All counterintelligence matters shall be referred to the Security Manager. The Security Manager will contact the nearest NCIS office as required.

c. The Security Manager is responsible for ISP security training, briefings and debriefings per Chapter 3 of reference (a).

d. The commanding officer does not have original classification authority per Chapter 4 of reference (a).

e. The Operations Officer is responsible for the review of classified information prepared in the command to ensure correct classification and marking. The Operations Officer will identify the sources of security classification guidance commonly used, where they are located, and promulgate to appropriate drafters using Chapter 6 of reference (a).

f. The safeguarding of classified information during working hours shall be conducted in accordance with Chapter 7 of reference (a). The reproduction of classified material is limited to working papers only and shall comply with reproduction limitations and any special controls placed on information by originators.

g. The transportation of classified material requires a courier card signed by the Security Manager with the exception of burn bag destruction. Burn bag destruction requires two personnel to maintain proper control and documentation. The transporting of classified material will be conducted in accordance with Chapter 9 reference (a).

h. The command Physical Security Plan, reference (i), is an integral part of the protection of classified material and should be used in close conjunction with this instruction. It includes other elements of command security including key and lock control and access to controlled spaces.

i. The command emergency destruction plan is reference (x).

j. Visitor control procedures, including clearance visit requests are conducted in accordance with reference (i).

k. Specified security functions may be performed for or by other commands using Security Servicing Agreements (SSAs), Memoranda of Understanding (MOU) or Memoranda of Agreement (MOA). Such agreements may be appropriate in situations where security, economy, and efficiency are considerations; e.g. burn bag destruction.

4. ACTION. The Security Manager is responsible for the following actions and reports.

a. A monthly report shall be submitted in Enclosure (1) format to the Commanding Officer no later than five working days after the end of the month.

b. The Information Security Program Assignments shall be promulgated quarterly or upon transfer of designated personnel in Enclosure (2) format.

c. The security manager shall assess the vulnerability of the command classified information to loss or compromise during crew turnover or annually whichever is less. The Security Manager will evaluate and document the security posture of the command annually or after crew turnover. This assessment shall be conducted using Exhibit 2B of Reference (b).

d. Burn bags shall be serialized, inventoried monthly by radio personnel and accounted for in a log. The Security Manager shall spot-check the burn bag log quarterly or as required.

COMMANDING OFFICER

USS SHIP NOTICE 5510.36

Subj: INFORMATION SECURITY PROGRAM
ASSIGNMENTS

Ref: (a) SHIPINST 5510.36 *Information Security Program*

1. The following personnel are assigned Information Security Program position for USS SHIP:

Security Manager	LCDR XO
Security Officer	LCDR XO
Top Secret Control Officer (TSCO)	LT OPS
Top Secret Control Assistant	ITCS LCPO
EKMS Manager	LTJG COMMO
EKMS Alternate	LTJG ALTERNATE
EKMS Alternate	ENS ALTERNATE
Secret Control Officer	ENS CICO
Secret Control Clerk	OS3 CLERK
NWP Custodian	OS3 CUSTODIAN
NATO Control Officer	ENS CICO
Alternate NATO Control Officer	ENS ALTERNATE
Information Assurance Manager	ITCS LCPO
Information Assurance Officer	LTJG COMMO

(1 per information system and network in the command)

Security Assistant	YN1 YEOMAN

2. This Notice shall be revised quarterly or as required.

COMMANDING OFFICER

OPERATIONS SECURITY PAGE 13

ADMINISTRATIVE REMARKS

E-32

NAVPERS 1070/613

S/N 0106-LF-010-6991

SHIP OR STATION

USS SHIP (CG 99)

EMAIL AND INTERNET PRIVILEGES FOR USS SHIP PERSONNEL

1. Access to unclassified email and the internet for personal use is a privilege. The Commanding Officer can secure the use of unclassified email and internet access at any time for Operational Security reasons or bandwidth limitations. Unclassified email and internet surfing, as well as non-secure telephones (including cell phones) use are SHIP's greatest Operational Security (OPSEC) vulnerabilities.

2. OPSEC Critical Information (do not pass via email, on the internet, or over the phone):
   A. Times, dates, or places of current or future operations or port visits
   B. Style, methods, tactics, techniques or procedures used in operations (MIO, Escort, etc.)
   C. Ship's routines, including liberty expiration, mustering times, or watch rotations
   D. Ship's current or future employments
   E. Do not use personal "code" words or "talk around" Critical Information

3. By signing this page 13, you acknowledge the security risks to yourself and your ship-mates inherent in the use of non-secure communications, you are aware of information critical to OPSEC, and specifically what that information is. Any questions regarding OPSEC should be directed to the OPSEC team: Ops, SIWO, (and as determined by the command.)

4. Information cleared for release, such as newsletters approved by the Commanding Officer for the Public Affairs Officer or the OPSEC Officer may be provided to you. Do not elaborate or give details in addition to the released information such as style, methods, tactics, techniques or procedures used in operations; ship's routines, including liberty expiration, mustering times, or watch rotations, or similar information regarding our coalition partners.

5. Email, the internet, and cell phones are not private ways to communicate. Maintain OPSEC and encourage your family to do the same by not asking questions relating to the information above. OPSEC information is available from the OPSEC team to send to your family if you desire.

6. Violations of these guidelines will result in punishment in accordance with the UCMJ and a loss of phone, email and internet access. Loose lips sink ships.
By direction
O. P. S. Boss, LT, USN

- -

I hereby acknowledge the above NAVPERS 1070/613 entry and desire to have access to unclassified email and web-browsing privileges.

Signed: _____ Date: _____

NAME *(Last, First, Middle)*	SSN	BRANCH AND CLASS

13 ✷

TAILORED GLOSSARY

This tailored glossary is intended as a quick reference for terms encountered by an operations officer.

Part I: Messages and orders from higher headquarters

alert order. A planning directive that provides essential planning guidance and directs the initiation of execution planning after the directing authority approves a military course of action. An alert order does not authorize execution of the approved course of action. (JP 1-02)

ATO: air tasking order. A method used to task and disseminate to components, subordinate units, and command and control agencies projected sorties, capabilities, and/or forces to targets and specific missions. Normally provides specific instructions to include call signs, targets, controlling agencies, etc., as well as general instructions. (JP 1-02)

BPT: be prepared to. Acronym often used in WARNORDs.

COA: course of action. 1. Any sequence of activities that an individual or unit may follow. 2. A possible plan open to an individual or commander that would accomplish, or is related to the accomplishment of the mission. 3. The scheme adopted to accomplish a job or mission. (JP 1-02)

commander's intent. A concise expression of the purpose of the operation and the desired end state. It may also include the commander's assessment of the adversary commander's intent and an assessment of where and how much risk is acceptable during the operation. (JP 1-02)

CONOPS: concept of operations. A verbal or graphic statement, in broad outline, of a commander's assumptions or intent in regard to an operation or series of operations. The concept of operations frequently is embodied in campaign plans and operation plans; in the latter case, particularly when the plans cover a series of connected operations to be carried out simultaneously or in succession. The concept is designed to give an overall picture of the operation. (JP 1-02)

DIRLAUTH: direct liaison authorized. That authority granted by a commander (any level) to a subordinate to directly consult or coordinate an action with a command or agency within or outside of the granting command. Direct liaison authorized is more applicable to planning than operations and always carries with it the requirement of keeping the commander granting direct liaison authorized informed. Direct liaison authorized is a coordination relationship, not an authority through which command may be exercised. (JP 1-02) DIRLAUTH should be recognized as an opportunity for the granting of authority to exercise command by negation. Keep them informed.

EEFI: essential elements of friendly information. Key questions likely to be asked by adversary officials and intelligence systems about specific friendly intentions, capabilities, and activities, so they can obtain answers critical to their operational effectiveness. (JP 1-02)

EXORD: execute order. An order to initiate military operations as directed. (JP 1-02)

FRAGORD: fragmentary order. An abbreviated form of an operation order (verbal, written or digital) usually issued on a day-to-day basis that eliminates the need for restating information contained in a basic operation order. It may be issued in sections. It is issued after an operation order to change or modify that order or to execute a branch or sequel to that order. (JP 1-02)

interdiction. An action to divert, disrupt, delay, or destroy the enemy's military potential before it can be used effectively against friendly forces, or to otherwise achieve objectives. (JP 1-02)

interoperability. 1. The ability to operate in synergy in the execution of assigned tasks. 2. The condition achieved among communications-electronics systems or items of communications-electronics equipment when information or services can be exchanged directly and satisfactorily between them and/or their users. The degree of interoperability should be defined when referring to specific cases. (JP 1-02) Often discussed during planning for combined operations.

JFACC: joint force air component commander. The commander within a unified command, subordinate unified command, or joint task force responsible to the establishing commander for making recommendations on the proper employment of assigned, attached, and/or made available for tasking air forces; planning and coordinating air operations; or accomplishing such operational missions as may be assigned. The joint force air component commander is given the authority necessary to accomplish missions and tasks assigned by the establishing commander. (JP 1-02)

JFLCC: joint force land component commander. The commander within a unified command, subordinate unified command, or joint task force responsible to the establishing commander for making recommendations on the proper employment of assigned, attached, and/or made available for tasking land forces; planning and coordinating land operations; or accomplishing such operational missions as may be assigned. The joint force land component commander is given the authority necessary to accomplish missions and tasks assigned by the establishing commander. (JP 1-02)

JFMCC: joint force maritime component commander. The commander within a unified command, subordinate unified command, or joint task force responsible to the establishing commander for making recommendations on the proper employment of assigned, attached, and/or made available for tasking maritime forces and assets; planning and coordinating maritime operations; or accomplishing such operational missions as may be assigned. The joint force maritime component commander is given the authority necessary to accomplish missions and tasks assigned by the establishing commander. (JP 1-02)

joint force. A general term applied to a force composed of significant elements, assigned or attached, of two or more Military Departments operating under a single joint force commander. (JP 1-02)

joint operations. A general term to describe military actions conducted by joint forces, or by Service forces in relationships (e.g., support, coordinating authority), which, of themselves, do not establish joint forces. (JP 1-02)

JOPES: Joint Operation Planning and Execution System. A system that provides the foundation for conventional command and control by national- and combatant command–level commanders and their staffs. It is designed to satisfy their information needs in the conduct of joint planning and operations. The system is used to monitor, plan, and execute mobilization, deployment, employment, sustainment, and redeployment activities associated with joint operations. (JP 1-02)

maritime interception operations (MIO). Efforts to monitor, query, and board merchant vessels in international waters to enforce sanctions against other nations such as those in support of United Nations Security Council Resolutions and/or prevent the transport of restricted goods. (JP 1-02)

MTP: maritime task plan. A database of joint force maritime component commander (JFMCC)–approved tactical plans. The JFMCC ensures the database is integrated within the JFMCC organization, with other joint components, and with the joint force commander. The maritime task plan responds to maritime support requests, and considers tactical dynamics of the operational environment, scheme of maneuver, and apportionment for an operation.

objective. 1. The clearly defined, decisive, and attainable goal toward which every operation is directed. 2. The specific target of the action taken (for example, a definite terrain feature, the seizure or holding of which is essential to the commander's plan, or an enemy force or capability without regard to terrain features). (JP 1-02)

OPCON: operational control. Command authority that may be exercised by commanders at any echelon at or below the level of combatant command. Operational control is inherent in combatant command (command authority) and may be delegated within the command. When forces are transferred between combatant commands, the command relationship the gaining commander will exercise (and the losing commander will relinquish) over these forces must be specified by the Secretary of Defense. Operational control is the authority to perform those functions of command over subordinate forces involving organizing and employing commands and forces, assigning tasks, designating objectives, and giving authoritative direction necessary to accomplish the mission. Operational control includes authoritative direction over all aspects of military operations and joint training necessary to accomplish missions assigned to the command. Operational control should be exercised through the commanders of subordinate organizations. Normally this authority is exercised through subordinate joint force commanders and Service and/or functional component commanders. Operational control normally provides full authority to organize commands and forces and to employ those forces as the commander in operational control considers necessary to accomplish assigned missions; it does not, in and of itself, include authoritative direction for logistics or matters of administration, discipline, internal organization, or unit training. (JP 1-02) Compare to TACON.

OPLAN: operation plan. Any plan, except for the Single Integrated Operational Plan, for the conduct of military operations. Plans are prepared by combatant commanders in response to requirements established by the Chairman of the Joint Chiefs of Staff and by commanders of subordinate commands in response to requirements tasked by the establishing unified commander. Operation plans are prepared in either a complete format (OPLAN) or as a concept plan (CONPLAN). The CONPLAN can be published with or without a time-phased force and deployment data (TPFDD) file. (a) OPLAN—An operation plan for the conduct of joint operations that can be used as a basis for development of an operation order (OPORD). An OPLAN identifies the forces and supplies required to execute the combatant commander's strategic concept and a movement schedule of these resources to the theater of operations. The forces and supplies are identified in TPFDD files. OPLANs will include all phases of the tasked operation. The plan is prepared with the appropriate annexes, appendixes, and TPFDD files as described in the Joint Operation Planning and Execution System manuals containing planning policies, procedures, and formats. (b) CONPLAN—An operation plan in an abbreviated format that would require considerable expansion or alteration to convert it into an OPLAN or OPORD. A CONPLAN contains the combatant commander's strategic concept and those annexes and appendixes deemed necessary by the combatant commander to complete planning. Generally detailed support requirements are not calculated and TPFDD files are not prepared. (c) CONPLAN with TPFDD—A CONPLAN with TPFDD is the same as a CONPLAN except that it requires more detailed planning for phased deployment of forces. (JP 1-02)

OPORD: operation order. A directive issued by a commander to subordinate commanders for the purpose of effecting the coordinated execution of an operation. (JP 1-02)

OPSEC: operations security. A process of identifying critical information and subsequently analyzing friendly actions attendant to military operations and other activities to: (a) identify those actions that can be observed by adversary intelligence systems; (b) determine indicators that hostile intelligence systems might obtain that could be interpreted or pieced together to derive critical information in time to be useful to adversaries; and (c) select and execute measures that eliminate or reduce to an acceptable level the vulnerabilities of friendly actions to adversary exploitation. (JP 1-02)

planning order. A planning directive that provides essential planning guidance and directs the initiation of execution planning before the directing authority approves a military course of action. (JP 1-02)

PTDO: prepare to deploy order. An order issued by competent authority to move forces or prepare forces for movement. (JP 1-02)

RFF: request for forces. A formal request to higher headquarters to provide forces in addition to those planned in the TPFDD.

RFI: request for information. Any specific time-sensitive ad hoc requirement for intelligence information or products to support an ongoing crisis or operation not necessarily related to standing requirements or scheduled intelligence production. A request for information can be initiated to respond to operational requirements and will be validated in accordance with the theater command's procedures. (JP 1-02)

ROE: rules of engagement. Directives issued by competent military authority that delineate the circumstances and limitations under which U.S. forces will initiate and/or continue combat engagement with other forces encountered. (JP 1-02)

SOP: standing operating procedure. A set of instructions covering those features of operations which lend themselves to a definite or standardized procedure without loss of effectiveness. The procedure is applicable unless ordered otherwise. (JP 1-02)

supported commander. In the context of a support command relationship, the commander who receives assistance from another commander's force or capabilities, and who is responsible for ensuring that the supporting commander understands the assistance required. (JP 1-02)

supporting commander. In the context of a support command relationship, the commander who aids, protects, complements, or sustains another commander's force, and who is responsible for providing the assistance required by the supported commander. (JP 1-02)

TACON: tactical control. Command authority over assigned or attached forces or commands, or military capability or forces made available for tasking, that is limited to the detailed direction and control of movements or maneuvers within the operational area necessary to accomplish missions or tasks assigned. Tactical control is inherent in operational control. Tactical control may be delegated to, and exercised at any level at or below the level of combatant command. When forces are transferred between combatant commands, the command relationship the gaining commander will exercise (and the losing commander will relinquish) over these forces must be specified by the Secretary of Defense. Tactical control provides sufficient authority for controlling and directing the application of force or tactical use of combat support assets within the assigned mission or task. Compare with OPCON.

TPFDD: time-phased force and deployment data. The Joint Operation Planning and Execution System database portion of an operation plan; it contains time-phased force data, non-unit-related cargo and personnel data, and movement data for the operation plan, including the following: (a) In-place units; (b) Units to be deployed to support the operation plan with a priority indicating the desired sequence for their arrival at the port of debarkation; (c) Routing of forces to be deployed; (d) Movement data associated with deploying forces; (e) Estimates of non-unit-related cargo and personnel movements to be conducted concurrently with the deployment of forces; and (f) Estimate of transportation requirements that must be fulfilled by common-user lift resources as well as those requirements that can be fulfilled by assigned or attached transportation resources. (JP 1-02)

UNODIR: unless otherwise directed. Often used in response to tasking from higher headquarters where discretion is left at the unit level or direction was unclear but time for clarification is limited. Use this response with caution, particularly with other services involved, as the Navy views orders expansively and the other services relatively restrictively.

WARNORD: warning order. 1. A preliminary notice of an order or action which is to follow. 2. A planning directive that describes the situation, allocates forces and resources, establishes command relationships, provides other initial planning guidance, and initiates subordinate unit mission planning. (JP 1-02)

Part II: Defining the battlespace

AOA: amphibious objective area. A geographical area (delineated for command and control purposes in the order initiating the amphibious operation) within which is located the Objective(s) to be secured by the amphibious force. This area must be of sufficient size to ensure accomplishment of the amphibious force's mission and must provide sufficient area for conducting necessary sea, air, and land operations. (JP 1-02)

AOR: area of responsibility. 1. The geographical area associated with a combatant command within which a combatant commander has authority to plan and conduct operations. (JP 1-02) 2. The specifically defined geographic or moving area around a naval force within an area of interest over which the officer in tactical command exercises all warfare responsibilities and controls tactical operations. The size and shape of the area are dependent upon the nature of the threat and the assets, both organic to the force or in dedicated support, available to counter that threat. (NWP 1-02)

contiguous zone. A contiguous zone is an area extending seaward from the baseline up to 24 nautical miles in which the coastal nation may exercise the control necessary to prevent or punish infringement of its customs, fiscal, immigration, and sanitary laws and regulations that occur within its territory or territorial sea. Ships and aircraft enjoy high seas freedoms, including overflight, in the contiguous zone. (NWP 1-14M)

EEZ: exclusive economic zones. A resource-related zone adjacent to the territorial sea—where a State has certain sovereign rights (but not sovereignty) and may not extend beyond 200 nautical miles from the baseline. Ships and aircraft enjoy high seas freedoms, including overflight, in the EEZ. (NWP 1-14M)

high seas. The high seas include all parts of the ocean seaward of the EEZ. (NWP 1-14M)

internal waters. Internal waters are landward of the baseline from which the territorial sea is measured. (NWP 1-14M)

littoral. The littoral comprises two segments of battlespace: 1. Seaward: the area from the open ocean to the shore which must be controlled to support operations ashore. 2. Landward: the area inland from the shore that can be supported and defended directly from the sea. (JP 1-02)

NAI: named area of interest. The geographical area where information that will satisfy a specific information requirement can be collected. Named areas of interest are usually selected to capture indications of adversary courses of action, but also may be related to conditions of the battlespace. (JP 1-02)

territorial seas. The territorial sea is a belt of ocean that is measured seaward up to 12 nautical miles from the baseline of the coastal nation and subject to its sovereignty. Ships enjoy the right of innocent passage in the territorial sea. Innocent passage does not include a right for aircraft overflight of the territorial sea. (NWP 1-14M)

waterspace management. The allocation of waterspace in terms of antisubmarine warfare attack procedures to permit the rapid and effective engagement of hostile submarines while preventing inadvertent attacks on friendly submarines. (JP 1-02)

Part III: Scheduling terms and abbreviations

ARR: Arrive port/place indicated between 0800 and 1100 local time. (NWP 1-03.1)

ASGN: Unit is operationally assigned to (name of command). (NWP 1-03.1)

ATENR: En route port/place indicated between 1100 and 1600 local time. (NWP 1-03.1)

COMPTUEX: Composite Training Unit Exercise. (NWP 1-03.1)

DLQ: Deck Landing Qualification. (NWP 1-03.1)

DSRA: Docking Selected Restricted Availability. (NWP 1-03.1)

EARR: Early Arrival port/place indicated between 0000 and 0800 local. (NWP 1-03.1) Compare with ARR.

Emergent Sked Change: The ship cannot meet the scheduled departure time and the time is changed prior to the planned departure period. For example, the day before a scheduled underway the ship suffers a major engine casualty and it cannot be repaired in 24 hours.

ENR: En route port/place indicated between 0800 and 1100 local time, or the entire day. (NWP 1-03.1)

ENRAT: Arrival port/place indicated between 1100 and 1600 local time. (NWP 1-03.1)

ESAIL: Early sail en route port/place indicated between 0000 and 0800 local time. (NWP 1-03.1)

Fail to Sail: The ship is scheduled to depart during a specific period and does not depart. For example, the ship is scheduled to depart at 0830 (ENR in Websked) and cannot get under way until 1200 due to heavy fog. The window for ENR is 0800 to 1100.

GRUSL: Group sail (similar ships together). (NWP 1-03.1)

HOLUPK: Holiday upkeep. (NWP 1-03.1)

INREP: Inport replenishment. (NWP 1-03.1)

IPT: In port. (NWP 1-03.1) (NOTE: INPT frequently used but incorrect.)

ISE: Individual Ship Exercise. (NWP 1-03.1) (NOTE: often translated as Independent Steaming Exercise.)

LARR: Arrival port/place indicated between 1600 and 2400 local time. (NWP 1-03.1)

LSAIL: En route port/place indicated between 1600 and 2400 local time. (NWP 1-03.1)

LVUPK: Leave and upkeep period. (NWP 1-03.1)

MLTSL: Multiple sail (dissimilar ship types sailing together). (NWP 1-03.1)

PASSEX: Passing exercise. (NWP 1-03.1) (NOTE: typically conducted with a foreign navy.)

PDUPK: Post-deployment upkeep. (NWP 1-03.1)

RFS: Readiness for sea period. (NWP 1-03.1)

SRA: Selected Restricted Availability. (NWP 1-03.1)

TYT: Type training. (NWP 1-03.1)

TYTIPT: Type training inport. (NWP 1-03.1)

UNREP: Underway replenishment. (NWP 1-03.1)

UPK: Upkeep. (NWP 1-03.1)

VST: Visit. (NWP 1-03.1)

WOWU: Week One Work-Ups. (SFTM)

XSOA: Excess speed of advance authorized. (NWP 1-03.1)

INDEX

Page numbers in *italics* indicate photographs.

ABOUT THE AUTHOR

JOHN CALLAWAY hails from Binghamton, New York. A graduate of Georgetown University, he was commissioned through the Navy Reserve Officers Training Corps in 1994. He served in six ships, including two tours as operations officer and two tours in command. Married with three children, he resides in Northern Virginia.